Street by Street

NUNEA....

ATHERSTONE, BEDWORTH, HINCKLEY

Ansley, Astley, Barwell, Bramcote, Bulkington, Burbage,
Earl Shilton, Exhall, Hartshill, Higham on the Hill, New Arley,
Sapcote, Sharnford, Stoke Golding, Stoney Stanton

CW00430198

1st edition November 2003
© Automobile Association Developments Limited
2003

Ordnance Survey® This product includes map data licensed from Ordnance Survey ® with the permission of the Controller of Her Majesty's Stationery Office. © Crown copyright 2003. All rights reserved. Licence number 399221.

Published by AA Publishing (a trading name of Automobile Association Developments Limited, whose registered office is Millstream, Maidenhead Road, Windsor, Berkshire SL4 5GD. Registered number 1878835).

Mapping produced by the Cartography Department of The Automobile Association. (A01723)

A CIP Catalogue record for this book is available from the British Library.

Printed by GRAFIASA S.A., Porto, Portugal

ML192

Key to map pages	ii-iii
Key to map symbols	iv–1
Main map pages	2-45
Index – towns & villages	46
Index – streets	47-54
Index – featured places	54-55
Acknowledgements	55

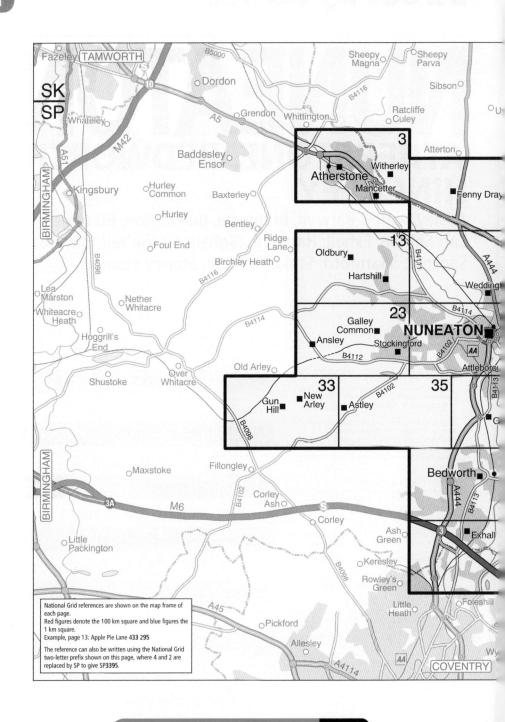

Fazeley TAMWORTH

B5000

Dordon

SK
SP

Whateley

A5   Grendon   Whittington

Sheepy
Magna   Sheepy
Parva

Sibson

Ratcliffe
Culey

M42

Baddesley
Ensor

B4116

Atterton

U

3

Witherley

Atherstone
Mancetter

Fenny Dray

BIRMINGHAM

Kingsbury

Hurley
Common

Baxterley

Hurley

Bentley

Foul End

Ridge
Lane

Birchley Heath

B4116

Oldbury

Hartshill

13

B4111

A444

Wedding

Lea
Marston

Whiteacre
Heath

Nether
Whitacre

B4114

Galley
Common

23

NUNEATON

B4102

AA

B4098

B4114

A51

A5

Hoggrill's
End

Ansley

Stockingford

B4112

Attleboro

Over
Whitacre

Old Arley

B4113

Shustoke

33

Gun
Hill   New
Arley   Astley

B4102

35

G

BIRMINGHAM

B4098

Maxstoke

Fillongley

Bedworth

A444

B4113

3A   M6

Corley
Ash

S

A444

3   Exhall

Little
Packington

Corley

Ash
Green

Keresley

B4098

Rowley's
Green

A45

Pickford

Little
Heath

Foleshill

Allesley

A4114   AA   COVENTRY   Wy

National Grid references are shown on the map frame of each page.
Red figures denote the 100 km square and blue figures the 1 km square.
Example, page 13: Apple Pie Lane **433 295**

The reference can also be written using the National Grid two-letter prefix shown on this page, where 4 and 2 are replaced by SP to give SP**3395**.

Scale of main map pages   **1:15,000**   4.2 inches to 1 mile

LEICESTER

SK
SP

LEICESTER

M1

B582

Peckleton

Kirkby
Mallory

Sutton
Cheney

ton

A447

Thurlaston

Enderby

M69

A47

Stapleton

Dadlington

7

9

Earl
Shilton

11

Narborough

Huncote

Littlethorpe

Stoke
Golding

Barwell

Elmesthorpe

Potters
Marston

Croft

Cosby

m on
Hill

17

B4668

19

B590

21

Stoney
Stanton

B4114

B581

Hinckley

A5

Nicolas
k

B4669

Sketchley

27

A47
eston
nge

29

Burbage

2

B4669

Sapcote

Aston
Flamville

Sharnford

31

Broughton
Astley

B581

Frolesworth

Leire

Dunton
Bassett

1

B578

7

Burton
Hastings

stone

Bramcote

39

M69

Wigston
Parva

B4114

43

Wolvey
Heath

Wolvey

B4114

Copston
Magna

Claybrooke
Magna

Ashby
Parva

A426

B4109

igton

B4112

Wibtoft

Ullesthorpe

B4109

B4065

B4112

B4455

Shilton

Withybrook

A5

Willey

Bitteswell

Lutterworth

Ansty

Monks
Kirby

B4027

A4303

Cotesbach

M6

Street Ashton

A426

2

A46

B4029

Stretton
under Fosse

B4027

Pailton

Churchover

A426

Shawell

LEICESTER

MAPI, THE SOUTH

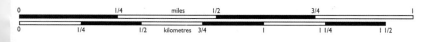

| 0 | 1/4 | miles | 1/2 | 3/4 | 1 |

| 0 | 1/4 | 1/2 | kilometres | 3/4 | 1 | 1 1/4 | 1 1/2 |

iv

Junction 9	Motorway & junction
Services	Motorway service area
	Primary road single/dual carriageway
Services	Primary road service area
	A road single/dual carriageway
	B road single/dual carriageway
	Other road single/dual carriageway
	Minor/private road, access may be restricted
← ←	One-way street
	Pedestrian area
	Track or footpath
	Road under construction
	Road tunnel
AA	AA Service Centre
P	Parking
P+	Park & Ride
	Bus/coach station
	Railway & main railway station
	Railway & minor railway station

⊖	Underground station
⊖	Light railway & station
+++++++++	Preserved private railway
LC	Level crossing
•—•—•—•	Tramway
----------	Ferry route
....	Airport runway
– · – · – · –	County, administrative boundary
ⱯⱯⱯⱯⱯ	Mounds
17	Page continuation
	River/canal, lake, pier
	Aqueduct, lock, weir
465 ▲ Winter Hill	Peak (with height in metres)
	Beach
	Woodland
	Park
	Cemetery
	Built-up area

Featured building

Abbey, cathedral or priory

City wall

Castle

Hospital with 24-hour A&E department

Historic house or building

Post Office

National Trust property

Wakehurst Place NT

Public library

Museum or art gallery

Tourist Information Centre

Roman antiquity

Seasonal Tourist Information Centre

Ancient site, battlefield or monument

Petrol station, 24-hour
Major suppliers only

Industrial interest

Church/chapel

Garden

Public toilets

Garden Centre
Garden Centre Association Member

Toilet with disabled facilities

Garden Centre
Wyevale Garden Centre

Public house
AA recommended

Farm or animal centre

Restaurant
AA inspected

Zoological or wildlife collection

Hotel
AA inspected

Madeira Hotel

Bird collection

Theatre or performing arts centre

Nature reserve

Cinema

Aquarium

Golf course

Visitor or heritage centre

Camping
AA inspected

Country park

Caravan site
AA inspected

Cave

Camping & caravan site
AA inspected

Windmill

Theme park

Distillery, brewery or vineyard

Dick's

E   F   G   H

32   33   99

I

Atherstone Road

Witherley Fields Farm

Ratcliffe Bridge

one Cricket

Ratcliffe Road

Works

2

98 Atterton

Lan

Carlyon Road Industrial Estate

ays

Mythe Lane

Lane

Atterton

3

Carlyon Road

4

Riversdale Road

Well Spring Close

A5

Industrial Estate

Mill Lane

Orchard Close

Witherley Hall Lane

Home Farm Close

Chapel Lane

Queen Elizabeth Lower School

Marie Close

Witherley United FC

Post Office La

Drayton Barn Farm

WITHERLEY ROAD

St Benedicts RC Primary School

Charles Road

Daniel Road

St Peter's Rd

Church Road

Witherley CE Primary School

Kennel Lane

Witherley

4

urch

Clover's Cl

The Spinney

Peter's Rd

St. Ptrs Rd

St. Peter's Close

Bridge Lane

Riverside

Hunt Lane

Hunter's Wk

297

ook Walk

Lewis Ct.

Priory Walk

HARPERS LANE

MANCETTER ROAD

Rantsden Road

WITHERLEY ROAD

A5

Barn Farm

ew Road

The Coppice

PO

B4111

MANCETTER RD

Mancetter

5

Victoria Rd

Old Farm Road

Findley Cl

Manor House

Mill La

Lodge Cl

32   33

E   F   G   H

NUNE

Garden Centre

Crab Tree Farm

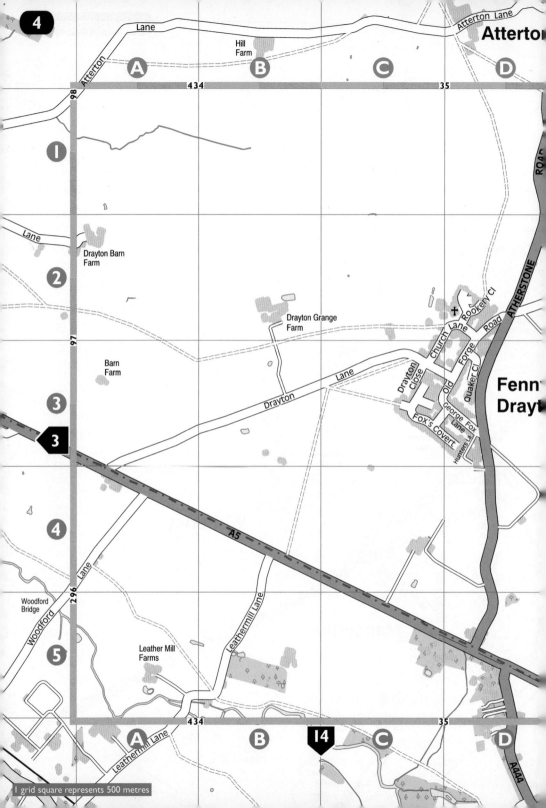

CV13

E F G H Upton Park
I
Lodge Farm
Stoke Road
Fenn Lanes
Hill Farm
White Gables Farm
Lanes
Ashpole Spinney
2
97
3
6
Proving
4
Rowden House Farm
Lindley Hall Farm
5
296
Station Road
36 37
E A5 F 15 G H Wood Lane
Mira Drive
Mira Dr
Lindley Grange
Higha

A B C D

438 39

Upton
Park

Fenn Lanes

Fenn Lane
Farm

Foxcovert Lane

Grange
Farm

CV13

Foxcovert
Farm

Upton Lane

Willow Park
Industrial Est

Station

Brook
Farm

Higham
Fields

5

Higham Lane

Proving
Ground

Stoke Lane

Station Road

Hilary
Bevins
Close

Stoke Lane

✝ Higham on the Hill
Primary School

Wood Lane

Main Street

PO ✝

Hinckley Lane

438 39

A B 16 C D

1 2 3 4 5

98 97 96

1 grid square represents 500 metres

Higham on

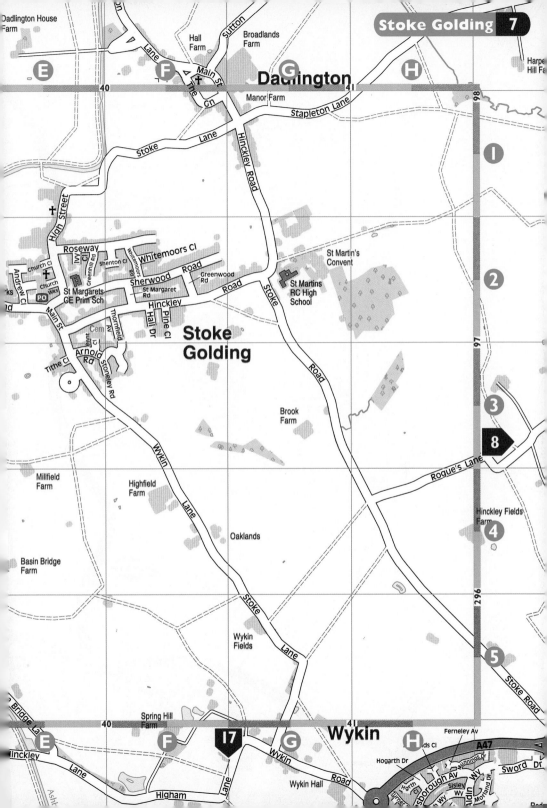

Dadlington House Farm

Hall Farm

Broadlands Farm

Sutton Lane

Main St

The Gn

Dadlington

Manor Farm

Stapleton Lane

Stoke Lane

Hinckley Road

High Street

Roseway

Ivy Cl

Whitemoors Cl

Shenton Cl

Greenhill Rd

Whitemoors Rd

Sherwood Rd

St Margaret Rd

Greenwood Rd

Church Cl

Andrew Cl

Church Wks

PO

St Margarets CE Prim Sch

Hinckley

Thornfield Av

Hall Dr

Pine Cl

Cem

St Martin's Convent

St Martins RC High School

Stoke Road

Stoke Golding

Main St

Arnold Rd

Stoneley Rd

Tithe Cl

Brook Farm

Rogue's Lane

8

Millfield Farm

Highfield Farm

Oaklands

Hinckley Fields Farm

Basin Bridge Farm

Wykin Lane

Stoke Lane

Wykin Fields

Stoke Road

Bridge La

Hinckley Lane

Spring Hill Farm

17

Wykin

Wykin Lane

Higham

Wykin Road

Wykin Hall

Ferneley Av

ds Cl

Hogarth Dr

A47

borough Av

Sisley Wy

Sword Dr

Morland Dr

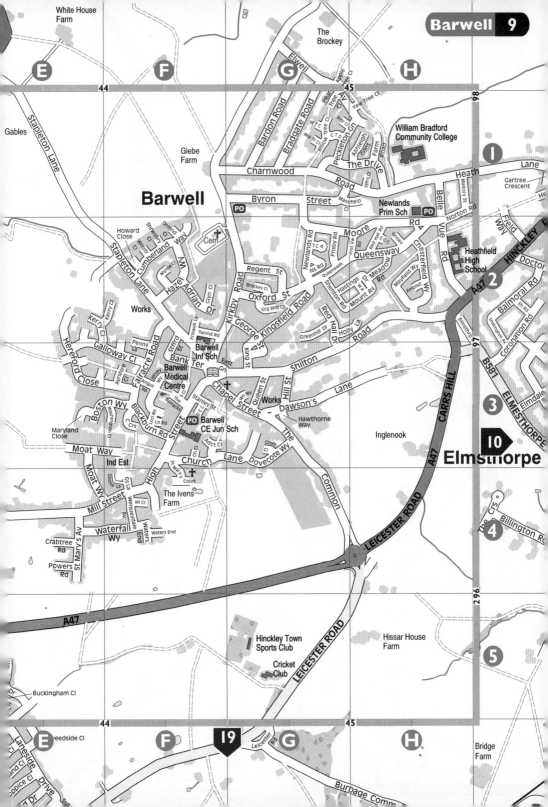

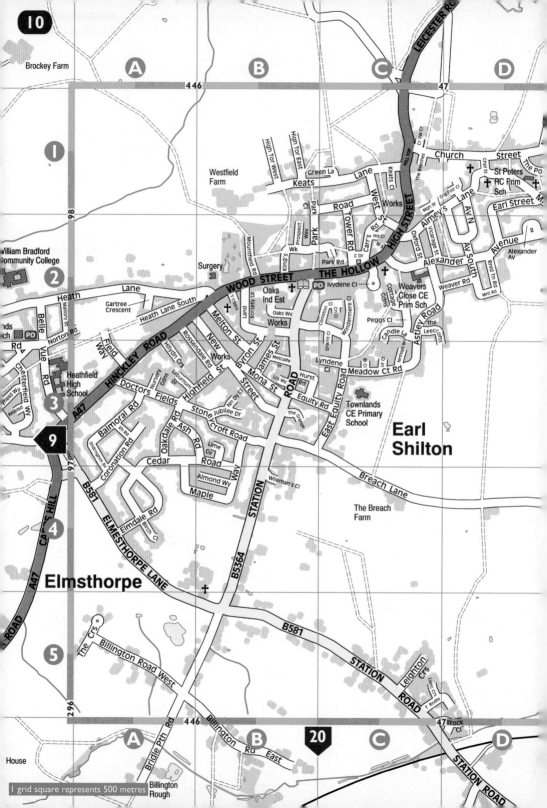

Dairy Farm

LE9

Normanton Turville

Earl Shilton Road

E 48 F G 49 H

I

8

Thurlaston Lane

King Richard's Hill

Fr B s

Water Gate Lane

2

Mirfield Farm

Pingle Lane

3

Mill Lane

M69

4

Huit Farm

Lane

97

296

5 Po Ma

Thorney Fields Farm

Works

Pingle Lane

E 48 F 21 G 49 H

Sta

Huncote Road

12

A　430　B　C　31　D

1

Purley Chase Lane

Oldbury Farm

Works

Oldbury Reservoir

Wakeford

Arden Forest Estate

95

urley Chase olf Club

Ridge

Ridge Lane　**2**

Lane

Oldbur

If Course

enary Way

Lady Wood Farm

3

94

Oldbury Road

Pipers

4

Works

Lane

Ox Hayes Farm

COLESHILL

West View

ROAD

Centenary Way

St Johns Close

Limes Coppice

Centena

5

Ansley Hall

B4114

293　430　A　B　**22**　C　31　D

UNEATON ROAD

Manor House Farm

1 grid square represents 500 metres

Church End

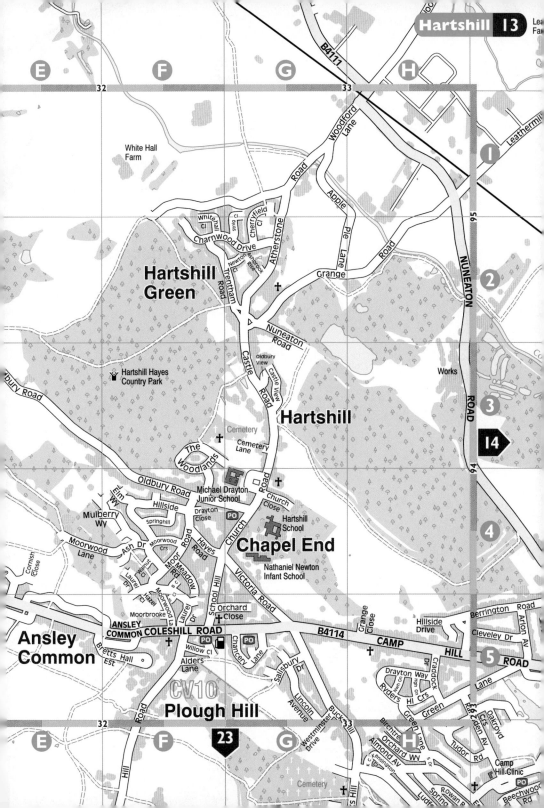

E   F   G   H

32   33

I

B4111

Woodford Lane

Leathermill

Lea
Fa

White Hall
Farm

Whitehall Cl

Cherryfield Cl

Cl Bldgs

Charnwood Drive

Atherstone Road

Apple Pie Lane

Grange Road

2

**Hartshill
Green**

Newton Greenbrook Rise

Trentham Road

Nuneaton Road

NUNEATON ROAD

96

3

Castle Road

Oldbury View

Castle View

Works

**Hartshill Hayes
Country Park**

Hartshill

I4

bury Road

Cemetery

Cemetery
Lane

The
Woodlands

4

Oldbury Road

Michael Drayton
Junior School

Drayton
Close

Road

Church
Close

ELM WY

Mulberry
WY

Hillside

Springhill

Drayton
Close

PO

Hartshill
School

Chapel End

Moorwood
Lane

Ash Dr

Moorwood
Crs

Moor Meadow Rd

Hayes Road

School Hill

Church Road

5

Cornish
Close

Walnut Cl

Laurel
Dr

Hazel Cl

Moorwood La

Laurel Dr

Nathaniel Newton
Infant School

Victoria Road

Grange
Close

Hillside
Drive

Berrington Road

Arion Av

Cleveley Dr

**Ansley
Common**

Bretts Hall
Est

Moorbrooke La

**ANSLEY
COMMON**

Orchard
Close

PO

Willow Cl

Alders
Lane

Chancery Lane

PO

Salisbury Dr

COLESHILL ROAD

B4114

CAMP

HILL

Lane

ROAD

Cradock Dr

Drayton Way

Ryders Hl Crs

Green

Craddock Green

Oakroyd Crs

Eaden Av

CV10

Plough Hill

Road

Hill

Lincoln Avenue

Buckhill

Westminster
Drive

Birchtree Rd

Orchard WY

Almond AV

Kensington

Tudor Rd

Camp
Hill Clinic

PO

E   F   G   H

32   33

23

Cemetery

Rowan R

Beechwood

Ludf

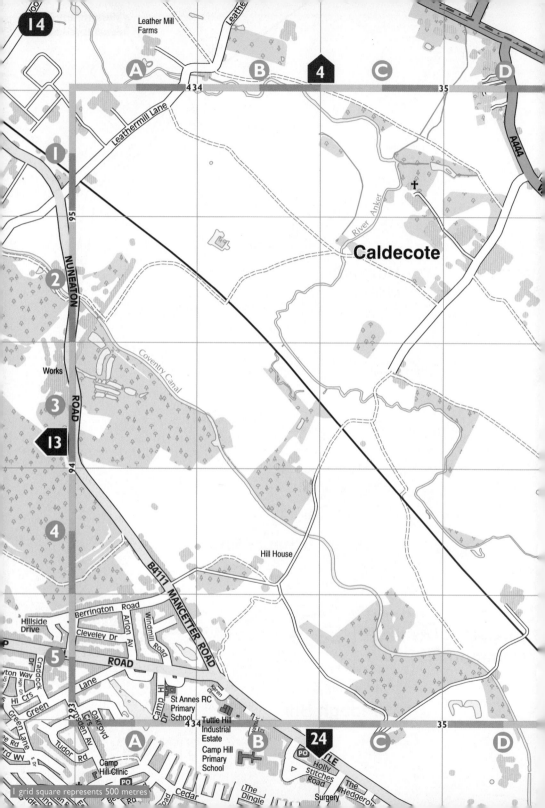

14

Leather Mill Farms

A
B
4
C
D

434

35

I

Leathermill Lane

A444

NUNEATON

River Anker

2

Caldecote

Works

Coventry Canal

3

ROAD

13

4

Hill House

B4111 MANCETTER ROAD

Berrington Road

Hillside Drive

Arion Av

Windmill Road

Cleveley Dr

5

ROAD

Craddock Dr

Green

Lane

St Annes RC Primary School

Tuttle Hill Industrial Estate

Camp Hill Primary School

Holly Stitches Road

24

PO

Surgery

A
B
C
D

434

35

Camp Hill Clinic

PO

The Dingle

Cedar

The Hedgerow

1 grid square represents 500 metres

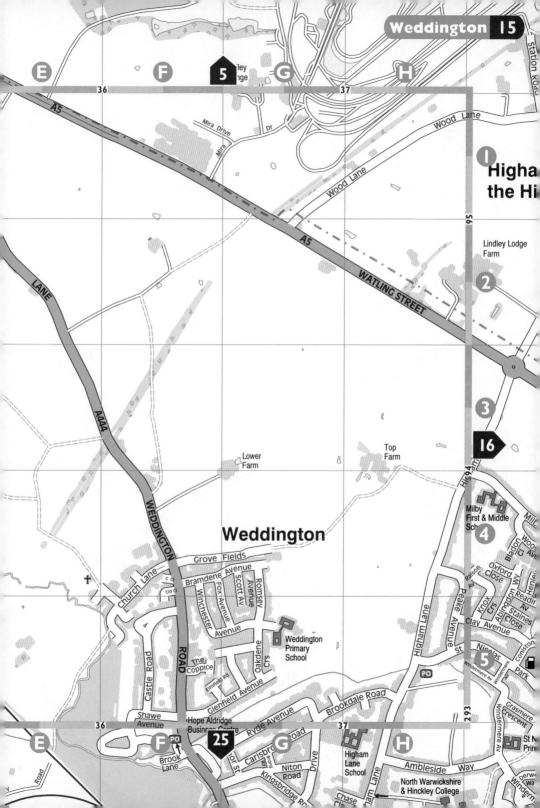

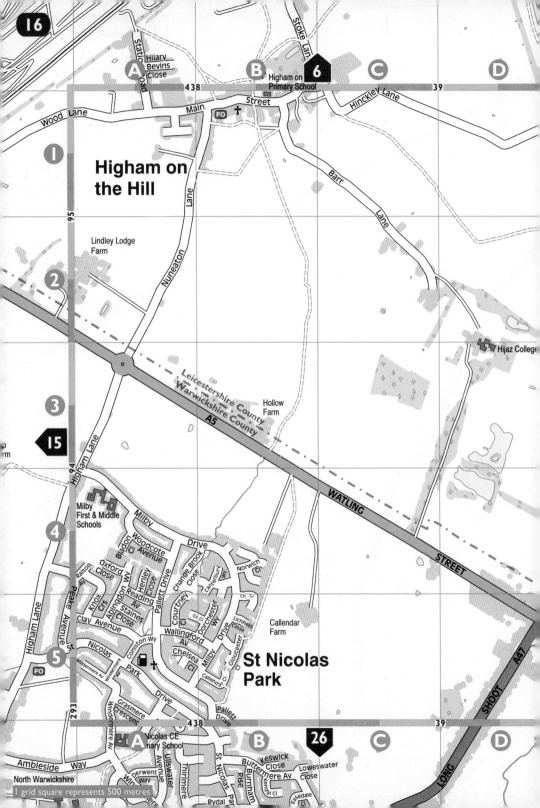

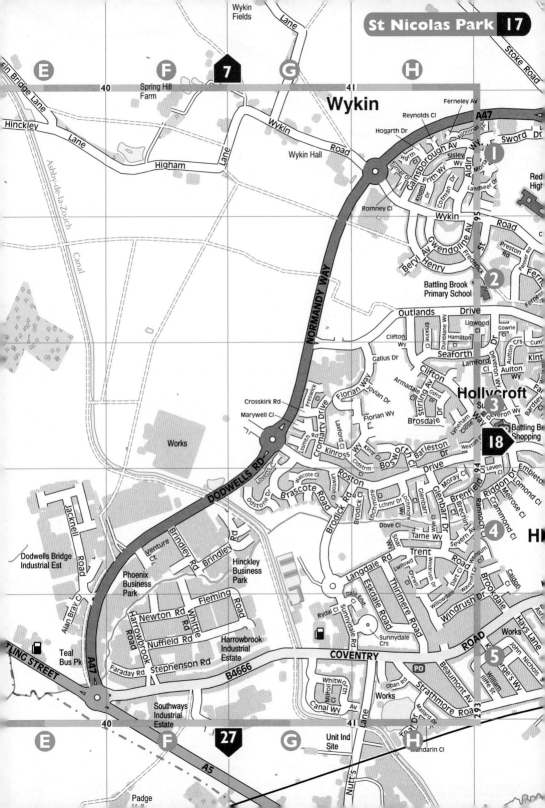

Stoke Road

7

E   40   F   G   41   H

Spring Hill Farm

Wykin

Wykin Fields

Lane

Wykin

Road

Ferneley Av

Reynolds Cl

A47

Hogarth Dr

Gainsborough Av

Running St

Sisley Wy

Sword Dr

Hinckley

Lane

Higham

Lane

Wykin Hall

Horth

Turner Wy

Frith Wy

Cotman Dr

Aldin Wy

Morla

Landseer Dr

I

Red High

Ashby-de-la-Zouch   Canal

Romney Cl

Kinson

St

Wykin

Road

Preston Rd

Palmer Rd

Ferr

2

Gwendoline Av

Frederick

Beryl Av   Henry

Battling Brook Primary School

Outlands

Drive

Linwood Cl

Gowrie

Dr

Cum

Clifton Wy

Erskine Cl

Dunblane Wy

Hamilton Cl

Seaforth

Aulton Crs

Kint

Gallus Dr

Clifton Av

Lamford Cl

Deveron Dr

Aulton

Crosskirk Rd

Freswick

Cronarty Drive

Florian Way

Jovian Dr

Stirling

Gsfrd

Armadale

Rd

Hollycroft

Deveron Wy

Su

3

Marywell Cl

Florian Wy

Brosdale

Lyneham

Close Wy

Weston

Battling B Shopping

18

Lssmth's Rd

Lanford

Klmr Cl

Wy

Cldstrm

Bosworth

Barleston

Cl

Moray Cl

Leven Cl

Embleto

Kinross

Lovett's Cl

Lawton Dr

Roston

Rd

Brodick Rd

Drive

Brenfield

Riddon Dr

Melrose Cl

Lomond Cl

94

Odstone Dr

Nalcote Cl

Brascote

Road

Lchmr Dr

Lochmore

Glenbarr Dr

Brechin

Crammond Cl

Rannoch Cl

4

Dove Cl

Tame Wy

Glenbarr

 Id akm

Severn Av

Works

Jacknell

Road

Venture Ct

Brindley Rd

Brindley Road

Hinckley Business Park

Trent

Soar

Lwnswd

Chrwll

Windrush Dr

Dart cl

Wensum

Waveney cl

Calden

H

Dodwells Bridge Industrial Est

Phoenix Business Park

Fleming

Road

Langdale Rd

Eskdale Road

Thirlmere Road

Brookdale

Road

Works

Hays Lane

Alan Bray Cl

Newton Rd

Whittle

Dr

Harrowbrook   Road

Nuffield Rd

Harrowbrook Industrial Estate

Dale End

Rydal Cl

Sunnydale Rd

COVENTRY

John Nichols

George's Wy

William St

Iliffe St

5

TLING STREET

Teal Bus Pk

Faraday Rd

Stephenson Rd

B4666

Sunnydale Crs

Beaumont Av

Strathmore Road

Works

A47

Southways Industrial Estate

Whitworth Cl

Milford Cl

Canal Wy

Oban Av

PO

Mallard Dr

ROAD

40   E   F   **27**   G   41   H

Unit Ind Site

Nutt's Lane

Mandarin Cl

A5

Padge

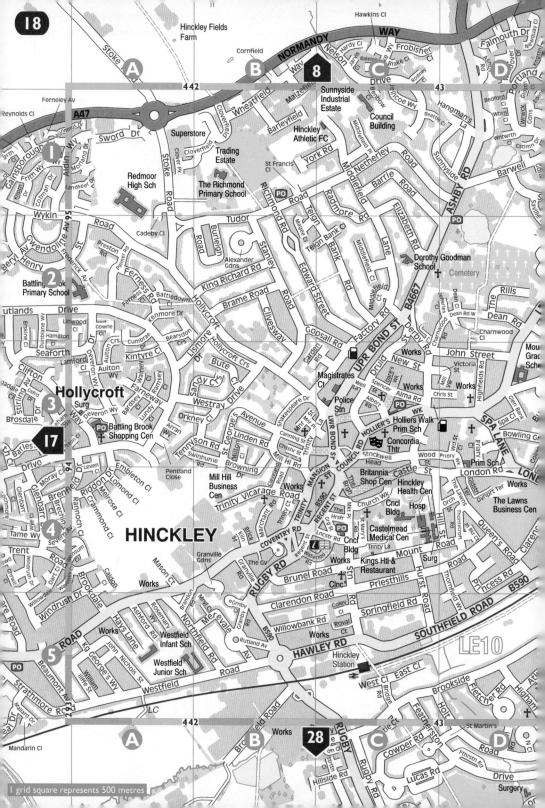

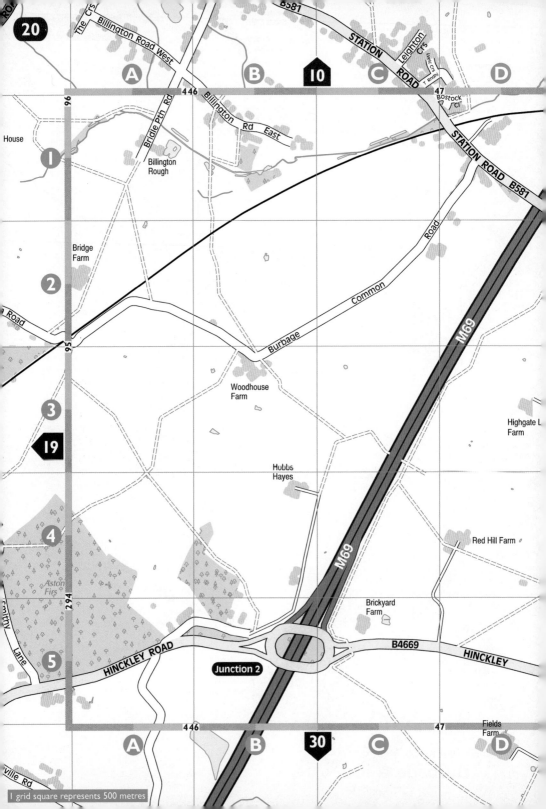

Stoney Stanton

Sapcote

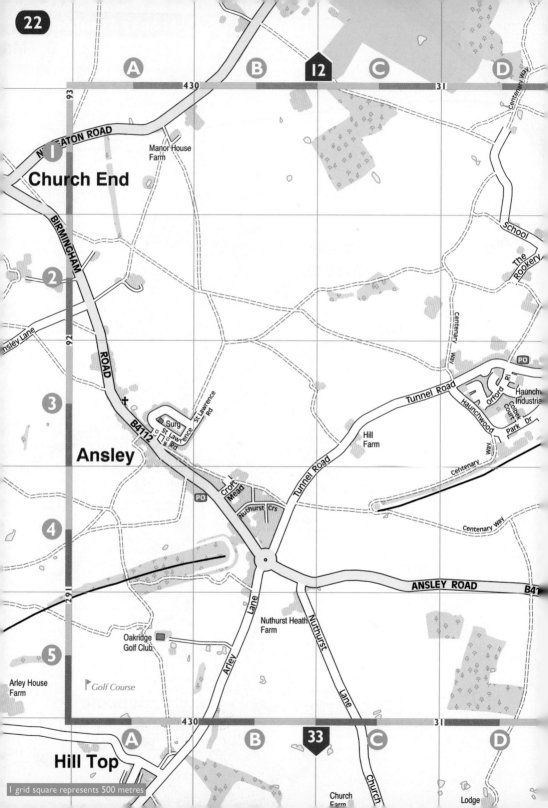

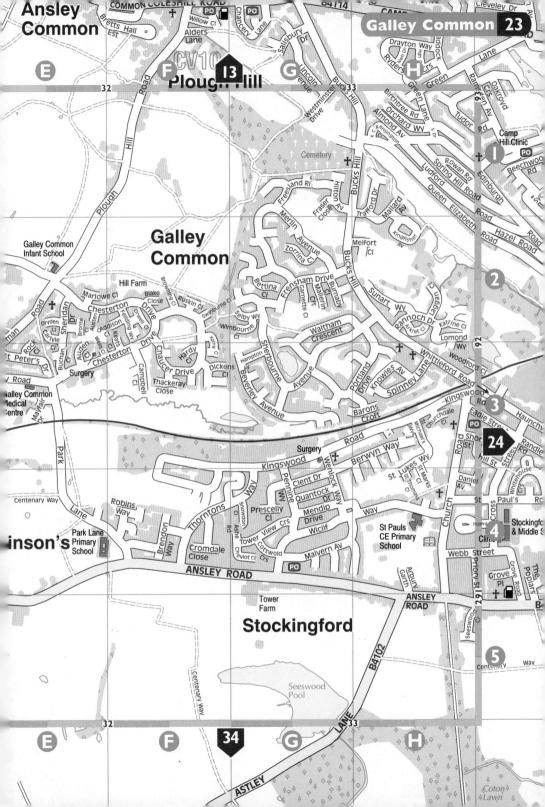

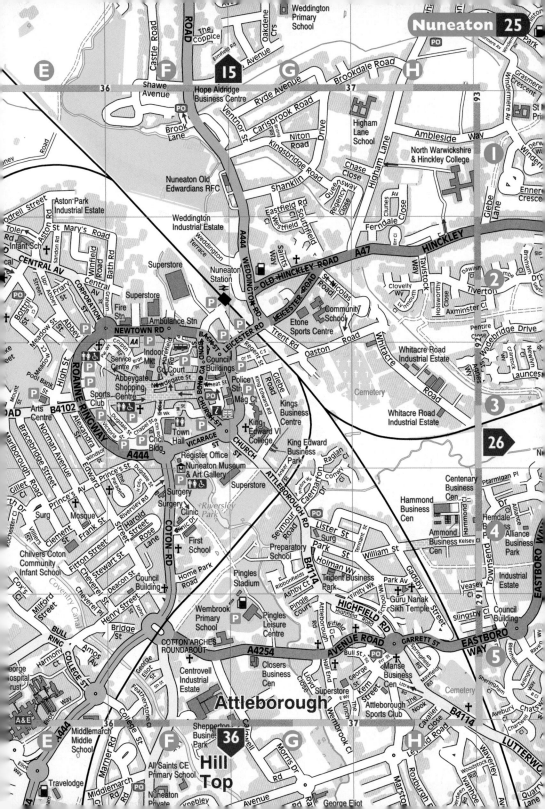

St Nicolas Park

26
PO

A
B
16
C
D

St Nicolas CE Primary School

North Warwickshire & Hinckley College

Ambleside Way

Windermere Avenue

Derwent Way

Keswick Close
Loweswater Close
Buttermere Av
Burnham
Kendal Cl
Easedale

Grasmere Crescent
Con12ton Wy
Nicolas
Park
Drive
Milby
Gloucester
Cl
Callendar
Cl
Chelsea
Cl
Pallett Drive
438
39

Ullswater Avenue
Thirlmere Av
St Nicolas Rise
St Nicolas Park Dr
Langdale Drive
Rydal Av
Skelwith
Ri
Travelodge

Ennerdale Crescent
Ensor Cl

HINCKLEY ROAD
438
93
92

Tavistock Way
Holsworthy Close
Axminster Cl
Tiverton

2
Dawlish Cl
Salcombe
Brixham
Sidmouth Cl
Creedon
Seaton Cl
Truro Cl
Camborne
Falmouth Cl
Newquay
Liskeard Close
Sennen Close
Tintagel Drive
Hayle

Horeston Grange Shopping Cen
PO

Horeston Grange

THE LONG SHY
A47

Wadebridge Drive
Pentire Close
St Agnes Wy
Cranock
Newlyn
Penzance Way
Padstow
Kelston
St Ives Wy
Lamorna
Camborne Drive
Redruth Close
Predryn
Launceston Drive

EASTBORO WAY

Hemdale

Wheatcroft Farm

Whitacre Road Industrial Estate

Road
92

3
Acre Road Industrial Estate

25

Nuneaton RFC

A4254

Ptarmigan Pl
Liberty Wy

4
Centenary Business Cen
Hammond Business Cen
Amm Business Cen
Kelsey Cl
Townsend
Drummond
Veasey
29

Hemdale Business Park
Alliance Business Park
Industrial Estate

Heart of England Crematorium

River Anker
Paul's Ford

Slingsby Cl
Council Building

Nanak Temple

EASTBORO WAY

Garrett St
5

Surgery
Raven
Blenmore
Holly Walk
Crowhill Drive
Ashleton Dr
Arlington Way
Sheringham
Avebury
Chatsworth Wy
Charnwood
Aldermoor
Woodhall Cl
Stainforth
Ragley Cl
Bramble Cl
Hebden Wy
Woodhall
Grassington Drive
Malham Close
Aysgarth Close
Ingleton Road
Leyburn Close

Hill Farm

Cemetery
Mayfield Rd
Cavalier Road
Leyland Road
Woodstock Rd
B4114
Waverley Rd
Roxb

LUTTERWORTH ROAD

A
Rosewood
Rainsbrook Drive
Leam Cl
Inchford Cl
Pickford Cl
Alderbrooke Dr
Aster Cl
B
Oberon Close
Wentworth
Aldrb Dr
37
Shakespeare
Juliet
Carthaway Dr
Verona Cl
Hoylake Close
C
St Andrews Dr
Dowsing
Golf Course
D

1 grid square represents 500 metres

19

E
F
G
H

Rd

Hastings
High School

St Catherine's

Fairway

Works

Woodbank

Banky Mdw

Winchester Dr

Mnlprgn

Winchester Dr

Dorchester Rd

Hinckley

Hinckley

nnyhill

Sunnyhill S

44
Road

Forresters

Balliol Rd

Woodland Avenue

The Nook

Salisbury Rd

45

Lyndhurst Cl

Ashbrtn

Works

Sch Cl
Crossland
Row

Cambourne Rd

Ilminster
Cl

Burbage

Kestrel Cl

Crossland

HINCKLEY RD

B578

Aston La

De-La-Bere

Crs

Cottage
Farm

Cem

I

Love La

New
Rd

PO
CHURCH ST

Woodstock Cl

Grosvenor Crs

Poh's
Cl

Crs

Oak
Farm

Grove

Burbage
J&I Sch

Windsor St

Horsepool

Library
Lychgate Cl

Freeman's La

Lychgate Lane

Flamville Rd

2

92

Victoria Rd

Salem Rd

Britannia

Orch Cl

Works

Road

Lodge Cl

3

Bullfurlong La

Robinson Wy

Villa Cl

Workhouse Lane

30

LUTTERWORTH

Orchard
Farm

4

Bullfurlong
Lane

M69

Burbage
Fields

Workhouse La

Burbage
House

291

Hanover
International
Hotel & Club

ROAD

5

Leicester
Grange Farm

The
Lake

44
E

F

A5

45
G

B578

H

Ash-Pole
Spinney

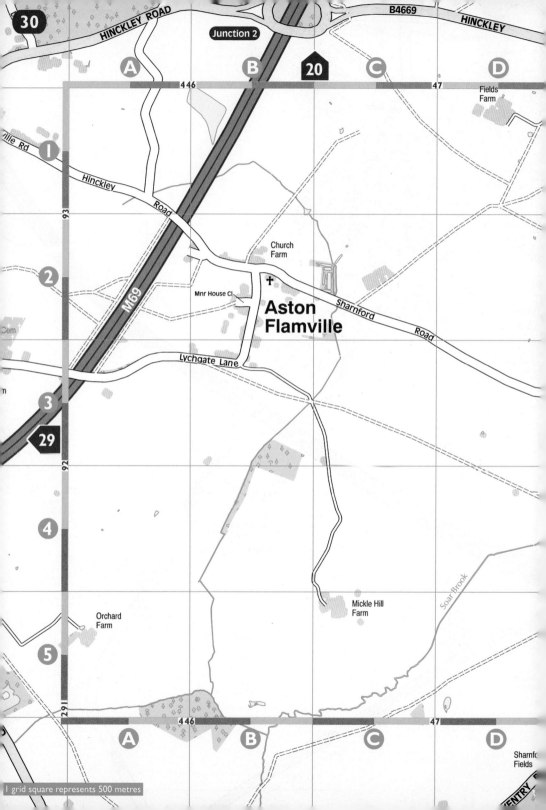

Stanton

ROAD

E

F

21

Hin

Frewen Drive

Park Road

Spa Drive

Penfold Close

Bui

Stanton Road

Kirby Close

Church St

G

Spa Drive

Harecroft Crescent

Underwood

Crs

Road

MIll Close

ckey Close

PO

SHpcote

Brown's Close

Livesey Drive

Nevill Smith Close

Church St

B4669 **LEICESTER**

ROAD

I

Castle Close

A S C

Wesley Cl

New Walk

Morley Rd

Calvert Crescent

Bassett Lane

Cook's Lane

Cem

All Saints CE
Primary School

Pougher Close

Sharnford Road

93

Springfield
Farm

2

ROAD

B

COVENTRY

River Soar

Ramsdale
Farm

3

Sharnford
CE Primary
School

Henson Way

Halls Crescent

Aston Lane

Holyoak Dr

Park

VIEW

Brookfield

Wy

Park Vw

Halls Crs

Chapel La

St Helen's Cl

B4114

Mill

92

Works

Works

LE10

Sharnbrook Gdns

Chapel St

ROAD

PO

Fx Hills

LEICESTER

4

Bungalow
m

Works

School La

Lees High

Fosse Cl

Sharnford

The Homestead

5

291

48

49

E

F

G

H

Cottage
Farm

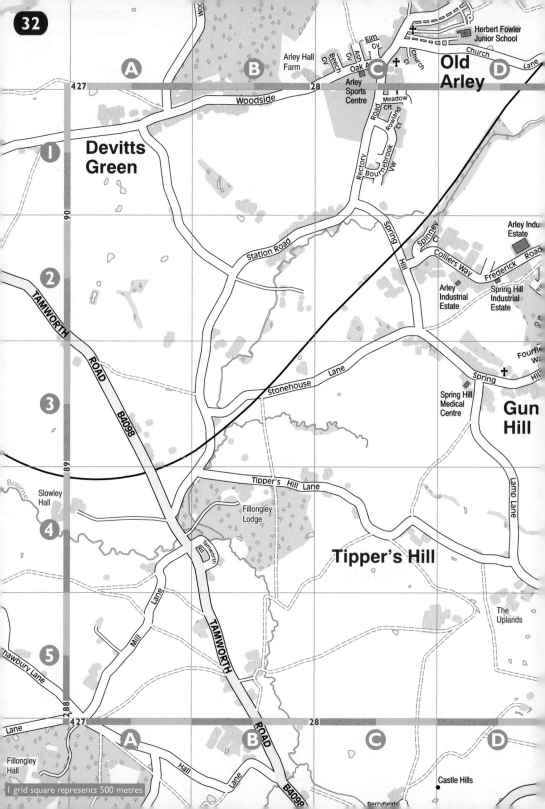

A **B** **C** **D**

Herbert Fowler
Junior School

Arley Hall
Farm

Beech Cv
Oak A
Ash A
Elm Cv
Church
Church Lane

**Old
Arley**

Woodside

Arley
Sports
Centre

Meadow

Cft
Rowland Cft

1

**Devitts
Green**

Rectory Road
Bournebrook Vw

Spring Hill

Spinney Cft
Colliers Way
Frederick Road

Arley Indu
Estate

Station Road

Arley
Industrial
Estate

Spring Hill
Industrial
Estate

2

TAMWORTH

Stonehouse Lane

Spring Hill

Fourfie
Wa

3

ROAD

B4098

Spring Hill
Medical
Centre

**Gun
Hill**

Bourne

Slowley
Hall

Tipper's Hill Lane

Lamp Lane

4

Fillongley
Lodge

Tamworth
Rd

Tipper's Hill

Mill Lane

The
Uplands

5

hawbury Lane

TAMWORTH

A **B** **C** **D**

Lane

ROAD

B4098

Fillongley
Hall

Castle Hills

Berryfields

Oakridge Golf Club

Arley House Farm

Golf Course

E **F** **22** **G** **H**

30 31

Hill Top

Church Lane

Church Farm

I

Lodge Farm

George Street
Ins St
Charles Street
Ransome Road
Gun Hill
PO
Hwrth Av
Sycamore Crescent
Lichfield Close
Gun Hill Infant School

New Arley

2

Astley Castle

Astley CE Sch

Astley

Nuthurst Lane
Castle Dr

3

Red Lane

34

B4

90 89

4

Windmill Lane

PARK LANE

B4102 PARK LANE

PARK LANE

B4102

Wood End

Howe Green

5

Wood End Lane

Green Lane

Cottage Farm

E **F** **G** **H**

30 31

88

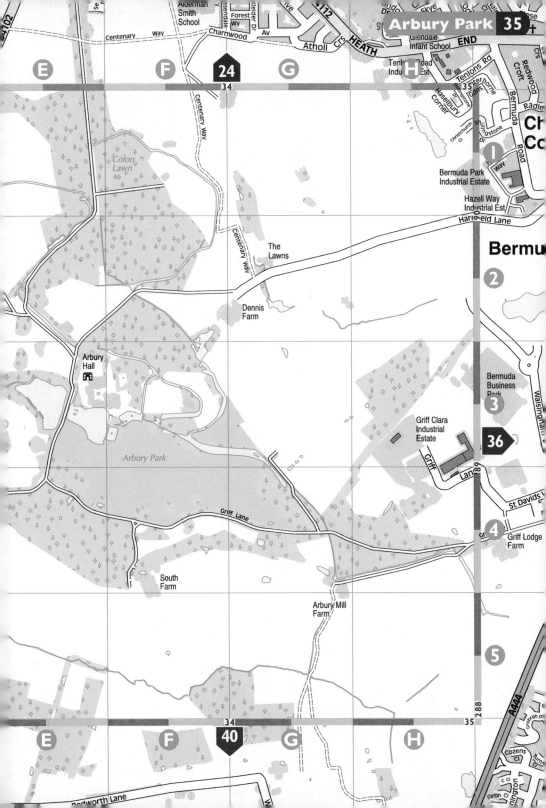

Alderman Smith School

Centenary Way

Charnwood

Forest Wy

Kielder Dr

Atholl

HEATH

Glendale Infant School

END

Tentons Road Indu Est

Christchurch Cl

Tentons Rd

Haselbury Corner

Redwood Croft

Bermuda

Radle

Ch Co

E

F

24

34

G

H

I

Coton Lawn

Centenary Way

Centenary Way

Bermuda Park Industrial Estate

Hazell Way Industrial Est

Harefield Lane

Bermu

The Lawns

2

Dennis Farm

Arbury Hall

Bermuda Business Park

3

Walsingham

Griff Clara Industrial Estate

36

Griff Lane

St Davids

Arbury Park

Griff Lane

4

Griff Lodge Farm

South Farm

Arbury Mill Farm

5

2 88

A444

E

F

40

34

G

35

H

Cozens Cl

Redworth Lane

Girtin

ington

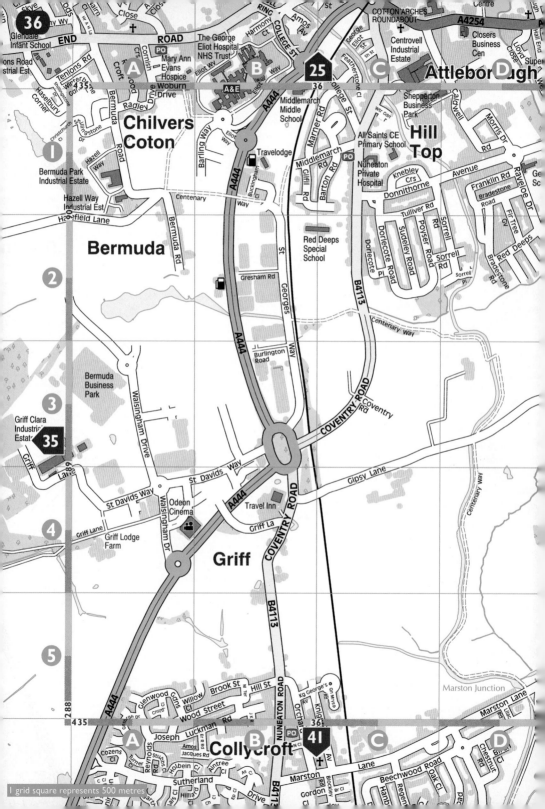

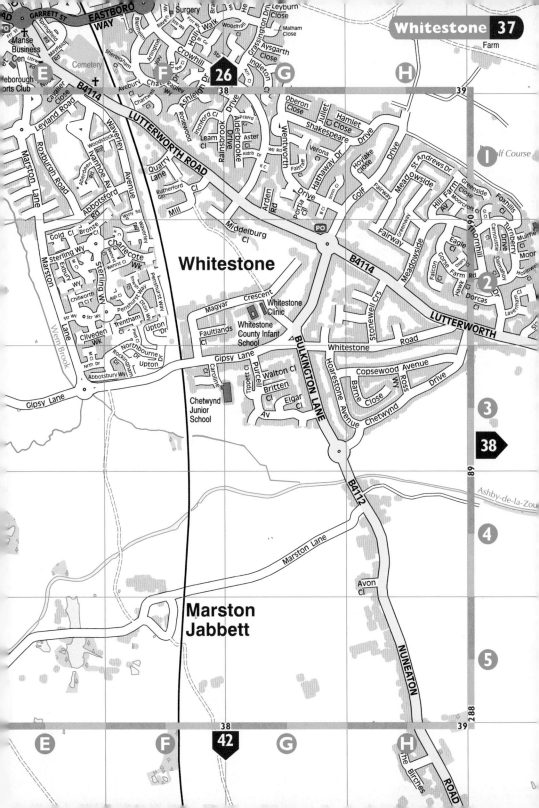

38

Hill Farm

A **B** **27** **C** **D**

439 40

Sinney Fields

Golf Course

1

Meadowside
St Andrews Dr
Greenside
Moorcroft Cl
Foxhills Cl
Hill Farm
Av
Thornhill
Turnberry Drive
Carnoustie Cl
Muirfield Cl
Nuneaton Golf Club
Greenway
Eagle Cl
Gorse Farm Rd
Thornhill Dr
Dalmahoy
Moorpark Cl
Hollinwell
Falcon Cl
Dorcas Cl
Lavender Cl

2

Meadowside

Mill La

LUTTERWORTH Road

ROAD

Ross Avenue
Drive
Slade Cl

Bramcote Hospital

3

37

Gorse Farm

B4114 LUTTERWORTH ROAD

Ashby-de-la-Zouch Canal

4

Beesley
William
Admirals Way
Dyers Road
Dyers Ccs
Alderney Cl
Hereford Rd
Whitch Rd
Artillery Rd
Cdl Lntro Knx Ccs
Grand Depot Rd
Bazza...
PO

Bramcote

5

NUNEATON
The Birch...
Rd

Gamecock Barracks

Bramcote Fields Farm

439 40

A **B** **43** **C** **D**

River Anke

E

F

28
42

Burton
Fields

G

H

Road 43

B4109

HINCKLEY ROAD

I

90

Townsends Cl

Hinckley Rd

Works

Cicey Lane

**Burton
Hastings**

Hinckley Road

Dents
Farm

Crossway
Farm

Burton
Fields

2

Abb
Fa

3

Shelford
Farm

B4109

Shelford House
Farm

Anker
Bridge

M69

B4114

Shelford

89

4

LUTTER

**Wo
Hea**

Shelford
Farm

TEMPLE HILL

Temple
Farm

5

Leicester

42

E

F

zzard Road

B4109

G

River Anker

H

Hall La

Hall Rd

Works 43

PO

CH HILL

The Square

COVENTR

Ch La

Croft Close

BULKINGTON ROAD

Wolvey CE
Combined

Fern

Orch Close

Dr

Wolds Lane

Loops

A   B   35   C   D

433
88
34

1

Astley Lane

Bedworth Lane

Cow
Lees

Woodlands

Dove
Cl

Lane

87

2

Bedworth
Woodlands

Woodlands

Road

Charles
Eaton Rd

Upp

Newtown Rd

Juniper
Cl

The Willows

Heather Dr

Erica

A444

3

Astley Hall
Farm

Astley Lane

Bedworth
Heath

The
Pines

The
Syms

The
Laurels

The
Alders

The
Symns

Croft
Rd

The Oaks

The Lawns

Wilder

Marriott
Rd

Coventry Way

Laburnum
Cl

Clandune
Wy

The
Limes

Silver
Birch

T Rwn

T Ch

Mp

Fern
Cv

Tfr

The
Beeches

Av

Road

Coventry Way

H Rd

Lindl
Rd

Primrose Dr

Bluebell Drive

Colu

LCl

The Wy

Foxglove
Wy

Brl

4

Ashington Road

Whitburn

Rd

Market End

Blyth
Cl

Cardigan Road

Tenby
Cl

PC

RRC

Newdigate
Primary
School

Anderson Road

Smercote Cl

PO

Smorrall

Lane

Bellairs

Av

Glebe Av

Martins
Rd

Renison

Heath

Rd

Alice Close

Alice

Holyhurst

Bescot

Road

Blair Dr

Mayor

Keenan Dr

Keenan Dr

Dark

Potters Rd

Kathleen
Av

PO

Cashmore

Hammersley St

Smith
St

Heatho

Holyoak
Cl

All Sms Rd

W W

River

Hospital

Goodyers
End

Newcomen
Cl

Raynor

Dowty

Howells

Newey
Av

Road

Robinson
Rd

Henson Rd

McMahon
Rd

Todp's
Drive

Smarts

Hayes Gn

Florence

Constance
Cl

Florence
Cl

5

Lane

Maynard
Av

Jeffrey
Close

Humphrey Dav

Cl

Melros
Av

Lane

End

Goodyers
End Primary
School

Bowling

Green

Lane

A444

St Giles
Junior
School

Robert

Moat
Dr

Farm

Acorn

Goodyers

M6

433
286

A   B   44   C   School   La   D

School

Startin
Road

High Cl

Startin
Cl

Bruc

Dal

ewland
all Farm

Breach Brook

Royal Oak Lan

Newland

1 grid square represents 500 metres

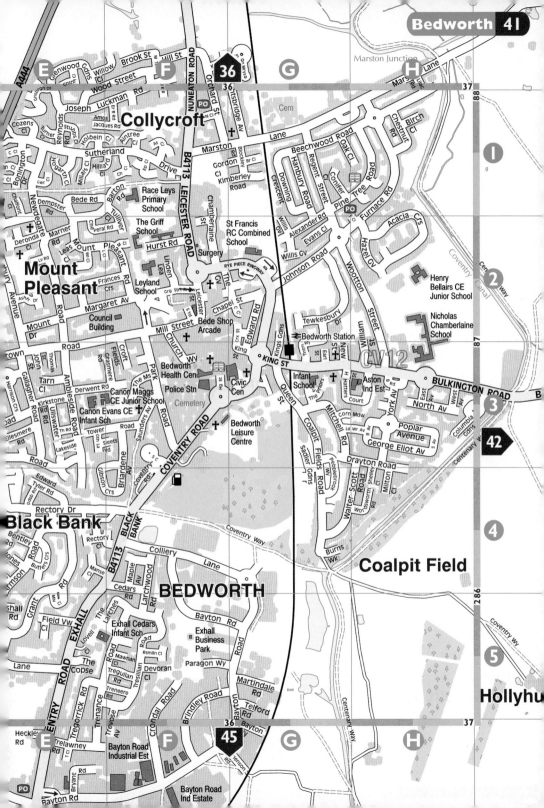

42

A B **37** C D

437 38

I

Weston Lane

Birch Cl

Coventry Canal

Centenary Way

Weston in Arden

Weston Hall Hotel

Weston

The Birches

Claremont Close

2

Hen
Bellair CE
Junior School

Nicholas
Chamberlaine
School

Mill Lane

Arden Forest
Infant School

The Paddocks

The

King

Clevelar

Severn Rd

Clyde Rd

Mersey Rd

Ribble

Calder

Larkin Cl

Hemsworth Dr

87

3

BULKINGTON ROAD

B4029

East
North Av

BEDWORTH ROAD

B4029

Trent

Tamar

Wye

Weston Lane

The Cft

Bedw

41

oplar
venue
ot Av

Centenary Way

Weston
Lawns
Farm

Bedworth
Road

Benn

Leyland Rd

Dingley Rd

B4109

4

286

ROAD

5

Coventry Wy

COVENTRY

Hollyhurst

437 38

A B C Top
Road D

LANE

I grid square represents 500 metres

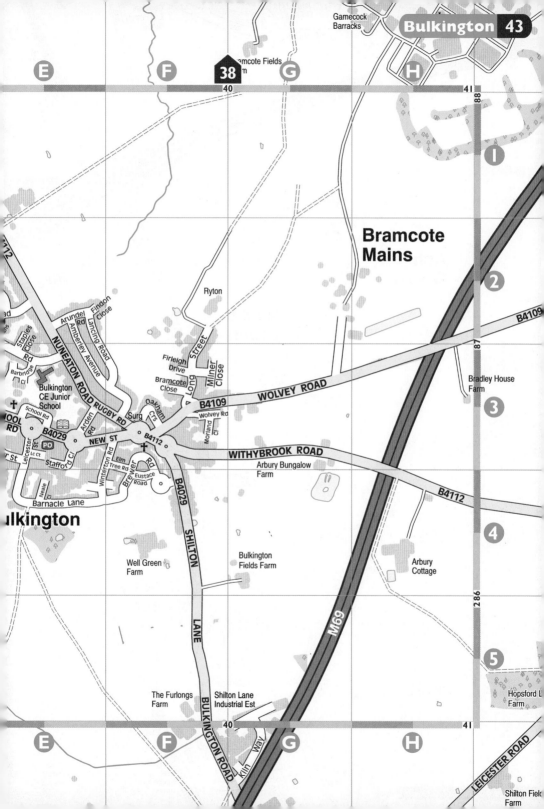

Gamecock
Barracks

E F G H

38

40 41

88

I

Bramcote Fields m

Bramcote Mains

Ryton

Arundel Rd
Findon Close
Amberley Avenue
Lancing Road
Staples Close
Barbnoe Cl
Rd

NUNEATON ROAD RUGBY RD

Bulkington
CE Junior
School

School Rd
SCHOOL RD

B4029

PO
SE
Lc Ct

Leicester

Arden Rd

Surg

NEW ST
Stafford Cl

Neale

Winterton Rd
Elm Tree Rd
Brewer Rd
Eustace Road

Barnacle Lane

lkington

Oakham Crs

Firleigh Drive
Bramcote Close

Milner Close

Long Street

B4112

Moriand Ct

B4109
Wolvey Rd

WOLVEY ROAD

B4109

87

2

Bradley House
Farm

3

WITHYBROOK ROAD

Arbury Bungalow
Farm

B4112

B4112

Arbury
Cottage

4

B4029

SHILTON LANE

Well Green
Farm

Bulkington
Fields Farm

2 86

5

Hopsford L
Farm

M69

The Furlongs
Farm

Shilton Lane
Industrial Est

BULKINGTON ROAD

Kiln Way

40 41

E F G H

LEICESTER ROAD

Shilton Fiel
Farm

1 grid square represents 500 metres

Alderman's Green 45 G4
Ansley 22 A3
Ansley Common 13 E5
Ash Green 44 A2
Astley 33 H3
Aston Flamville 30 B2
Atherstone 2 D1
Attleborough 25 F5
Barwell 9 F1
Bedworth 41 F5
Bedworth Heath 40 B3
Bermuda 36 A2
Black Bank 41 E4
Bramcote 38 C4
Bramcote Mains 43 H2
Bulkington 43 E4
Burbage 29 E1
Burton Hastings 39 E2
Caldecote 14 C2

Camp Hill 24 B2
Chapel End 13 G4
Chilvers Coton 36 A1
Coalpit Field 41 H4
Collycroft 41 F1
Devitts Green 32 A1
Earl Shilton 10 C3
Elmsthorpe 9 H3
Exhall 45 F1
Fenny Drayton 4 D3
Foxford 44 D4
Galley Common 23 F2
Goodyers End 40 A4
Griff 36 B4
Gun Hill 32 D3
Hall Green 45 F5
Hartshill 13 G3
Hartshill Green 13 F2
Higham on the Hill 16 A1

Hill Top 33 E1
Hill Top 36 C1
Hinckley 18 A4
Holbrooks 44 A5
Hollycroft 17 H3
Hollyhurst 42 A5
Horeston Grange 26 B2
Howe Green 33 H5
Longford 44 D4
Mancetter 3 F5
Marston Jabbett 37 F5
Mount Pleasant 41 E2
Neal's Green 44 B2
New Arley 33 F2
Normanton Turville 11 G1
Nuneaton 24 C4
Oldbury 12 D2
Plough Hill 13 F5
Robinson's End 22 D4

Rowley's Green 44
St Nicolas Park 16
Sapcote 21
Sharnford 31
Shelford 39
Sketchley 28
Stockingford 23
Stoke Golding 7
Stoney Stanton 21
Tipper's Hill 32
Weddington 15
Weston in Arden 42
Whitestone 37
Witherley 3
Wood End 33
Wykin 17

USING THE STREET INDEX

Street names are listed alphabetically. Each street name is followed by its postal town or area locality, the Postcode District, the page number, and the reference to the square in which the name is found.

Standard index entries are shown as follows:

Abbey St *NUN* CV11 ....**25** E2

Street names and selected addresses not shown on the map due to scale restrictions are shown in the index with an asterisk:

Abbeygate *NUN* CV11 * **25** F3

GENERAL ABBREVIATIONS

ACC ....ACCESS	E ....EAST	LDG ....LODGE	R ....RIV
ALY ....ALLEY	EMB ....EMBANKMENT	LGT ....LIGHT	RBT ....ROUNDABO
AP ....APPROACH	EMBY ....EMBASSY	LK ....LOCK	RD ....RO
AR ....ARCADE	ESP ....ESPLANADE	LKS ....LAKES	RDG ....RII
ASS ....ASSOCIATION	EST ....ESTATE	LNDG ....LANDING	REP ....REPUI
AV ....AVENUE	EX ....EXCHANGE	LTL ....LITTLE	RES ....RESERV
BCH ....BEACH	EXPY ....EXPRESSWAY	LWR ....LOWER	RFC ....RUGBY FOOTBALL C
BLDS ....BUILDINGS	EXT ....EXTENSION	MAG ....MAGISTRATE	RI ....F
BND ....BEND	F/O ....FLYOVER	MAN ....MANSIONS	RP ....RA
BNK ....BANK	FC ....FOOTBALL CLUB	MD ....MEAD	RW ....R
BR ....BRIDGE	FK ....FORK	MDW ....MEADOWS	S ....SOI
BRK ....BROOK	FLD ....FIELD	MEM ....MEMORIAL	SCH ....SCH
BTM ....BOTTOM	FLDS ....FIELDS	MKT ....MARKET	SE ....SOUTH E
BUS ....BUSINESS	FLS ....FALLS	MKTS ....MARKETS	SER ....SERVICE A
BVD ....BOULEVARD	FLS ....FLATS	ML ....MALL	SH ....SH
BY ....BYPASS	FM ....FARM	ML ....MILL	SHOP ....SHOPP
CATH ....CATHEDRAL	FT ....FORT	MNR ....MANOR	SKWY ....SKY
CEM ....CEMETERY	FWY ....FREEWAY	MS ....MEWS	SMT ....SUM
CEN ....CENTRE	FY ....FERRY	MSN ....MISSION	SOC ....SOCI
CFT ....CROFT	GA ....GATE	MT ....MOUNT	SP ....S
CH ....CHURCH	GAL ....GALLERY	MTN ....MOUNTAIN	SPR ....SPR
CHA ....CHASE	GDN ....GARDEN	MTS ....MOUNTAINS	SQ ....SQU
CHYD ....CHURCHYARD	GDNS ....GARDENS	MUS ....MUSEUM	ST ....STR
CIR ....CIRCLE	GLD ....GLADE	MWY ....MOTORWAY	STN ....STA
CIRC ....CIRCUS	GLN ....GLEN	N ....NORTH	STR ....STRI
CL ....CLOSE	GN ....GREEN	NE ....NORTH EAST	STRD ....STR
CLFS ....CLIFFS	GND ....GROUND	NW ....NORTH WEST	SW ....SOUTH W
CMP ....CAMP	GRA ....GRANGE	O/P ....OVERPASS	TDG ....TRA
CNR ....CORNER	GRG ....GARAGE	OFF ....OFFICE	TER ....TERR
CO ....COUNTY	GT ....GREAT	ORCH ....ORCHARD	THWY ....THROUGH
COLL ....COLLEGE	GTWY ....GATEWAY	OV ....OVAL	TNL ....TUN
COM ....COMMON	GV ....GROVE	PAL ....PALACE	TOLL ....TOLL
COMM ....COMMISSION	HGR ....HIGHER	PAS ....PASSAGE	TPK ....TURN
CON ....CONVENT	HL ....HILL	PAV ....PAVILION	TR ....TR
COT ....COTTAGE	HLS ....HILLS	PDE ....PARADE	TRL ....T
COTS ....COTTAGES	HO ....HOUSE	PH ....PUBLIC HOUSE	TWR ....TO
CP ....CAPE	HOL ....HOLLOW	PK ....PARK	U/P ....UNDER
CPS ....COPSE	HOSP ....HOSPITAL	PKWY ....PARKWAY	UNI ....UNIVER
CR ....CREEK	HRB ....HARBOUR	PL ....PLACE	UPR ....UP
CREM ....CREMATORIUM	HTH ....HEATH	PLN ....PLAIN	V ....\
CRS ....CRESCENT	HTS ....HEIGHTS	PLNS ....PLAINS	VA ....VA
CSWY ....CAUSEWAY	HVN ....HAVEN	PLZ ....PLAZA	VIAD ....VIAD
CT ....COURT	HWY ....HIGHWAY	POL ....POLICE STATION	VIL V
CTRL ....CENTRAL	IMP ....IMPERIAL	PR ....PRINCE	VIS V
CTS ....COURTS	IN ....INLET	PREC ....PRECINCT	VLG VILL
CTYD ....COURTYARD	IND EST ....INDUSTRIAL ESTATE	PREP ....PREPARATORY	VLS VI
CUTT ....CUTTINGS	INF ....INFIRMARY	PRIM ....PRIMARY	VW V
CV ....COVE	INFO ....INFORMATION	PROM ....PROMENADE	W ....W
CYN ....CANYON	INT ....INTERCHANGE	PRS ....PRINCESS	WD ....W
DEPT ....DEPARTMENT	IS ....ISLAND	PRT ....PORT	WHF ....WH
DL ....DALE	JCT ....JUNCTION	PT ....POINT	WK V
DM ....DAM	JTY ....JETTY	PTH ....PATH	WKS ....W
DR ....DRIVE	KG ....KING	PZ ....PIAZZA	WLS ....W
DRO ....DROVE	KNL ....KNOLL	QD ....QUADRANT	WY ....\
DRY ....DRIVEWAY	L ....LAKE	QU ....QUEEN	YD ....\
DWGS ....DWELLINGS	LA ....LANE	QY ....QUAY	YHA ....YOUTH HO

47

'OSTCODE TOWNS AND AREA ABBREVIATIONS

ıST ....Atherstone
ʌTH ....Bedworth
/E ....Coventry east
/N....Coventry north
HINC ....Hinckley
LUTT ....Lutterworth
MKTBOS/BARL/STKG ....Market Bosworth/ Barlestone/Stoke Golding
NUN....Nuneaton
NUNW/HART ....Nuneaton west/Hartshill
RCOVN/BALC/EX ....Rural Coventry north/ Balsall Common/Exhall
RLEIW/BAR ....Rural Leicester west/Barwell

Index - streets

Abb - Bri

A

ɔeygate *NUN* CV11 * 25 F3
ɔey Gn *NUN* CV11 * 25 E2
ɔey St *NUN* CV11 ....25 E2
ɔotsbury Wy *NUN* CV11 ....37 E3
ɔotsford Rd *NUN* CV11 ....37 E1
ɔotts Gn *HINC* LE10 ....29 E2
ɛles Wy *ATHST* CV9 ....2 B1
ɛrdeen Rd *NUN* CV11 ....37 E1
ngdon Wy *NUN* CV11 ....16 A5
'aham's Br *RLEIW/BAR* LE9 ....8 D1
ɪcia Crs *BDWTH* CV12 ....41 H2
ɪcia Rd *NUNW/HART* CV10 ....24 B2
ɪurch Cl *RLEIW/BAR* LE9 ....21 G2
ɪrn Cl *BDWTH* CV12 ....40 A5
:ote Cl *RLEIW/BAR* LE9 ....9 F3
ɪison Cl *NUNW/HART* CV10 ....23 E2
mirals Wy *NUN* CV11 ....38 C4
ɪian Dr *RLEIW/BAR* LE9 ....9 F2
ɪians' Cl *ATHST* CV9 ....3 E5
sdale Cl *COVN* CV6 ....45 F4
tree Cl *BDWTH* CV12 ....41 F1
n Bray Cl *HINC* LE10 ....17 E5
ert Rd *HINC* LE10 ....18 C3
ert St *NUNW/HART* CV10 ....24 B4
righton Wk *NUN* CV11 ....26 B5
erbrooke Dr *NUN* CV11 ....37 G1
erman's Green Rd *COVE* CV2 ....45 F5
er Meadow Cl *COVN* CV6 ....44 B5
erney Cl *NUN* CV11 ....38 D4
ers La *NUNW/HART* CV10 ....13 F5
Alders *BDWTH* CV12 ....40 C3
n Wy *HINC* LE10 ....17 H1
'idge Rd *HINC* LE10 ....28 C1
worth Dr *HINC* LE10 ....28 D3
ɪander Av *RLEIW/BAR* LE9 ....10 D2
ɪander Gdns *HINC* LE10 ....18 B2
ɪander Rd *BDWTH* CV12 ....41 G2
ɪandra St *NUN* CV11 ....25 E3
eton Cl *HINC* LE10 ....29 E2
e Cl *BDWTH* CV12 ....40 D4
on Sq *COVE* CV2 ....45 F4
ɪnce Cl *NUN* CV11 ....26 A4
aints Cl *RLEIW/BAR* LE9 ....31 G1
aints Rd *BDWTH* CV12 ....40 D4
a Rd *HINC* LE10 ....18 C3
ey's La *RLEIW/BAR* LE9 ....10 C2
ond Av *NUNW/HART* CV10 ....23 H1
ond Wy *RLEIW/BAR* LE9 ....10 B4
ɔerley Av *BDWTH* CV12 ....43 E2
ɔien Rd *ATHST* CV9 ....2 C4
ɔion Wy *HINC* LE10 ....19 E3
leside *RLEIW/BAR* LE9 ....9 H2
leside Rd *BDWTH* CV12 ....41 E3
ɔleside Wy *NUN* CV11 ....25 H1
s Av *NUNW/HART* CV10 ....25 E5
ɔs Jacques Rd *BDWTH* CV12 ....41 E1
Cl *COVN* CV6 ....44 D4
erton Rd *BDWTH* CV12 ....40 A4
OVN CV6 ....45 F4
rew Cl
KTBOS/BARL/STKG CV13 ....7 E2
us Rd *RLEIW/BAR* LE9 ....9 F3
er Br *NUN* CV11 ....39 E4
er St *NUN* CV11 ....25 G4
ll Dr *COVN* CV6 ....45 E3
ey Common
UNW/HART CV10 ....13 F5
ey Rd *NUNW/HART* CV10 ....22 C4
UNW/HART CV10 ....23 H5
lebee Rd *HINC* LE10 ....28 B1
le Pie La *NUNW/HART* CV10 ....13 G1
ry Av *BDWTH* CV12 ....41 E2
ry Garth *NUNW/HART* CV10 ....23 H4
ry Rd *NUNW/HART* CV10 ....24 A5
n Av *ATHST* CV9 ....2 D3
n Rd *BDWTH* CV12 ....43 E3
UN CV11 ....37 G1
n St *ATHST* CV9 ....2 D4
et Cl *NUNW/HART* CV10 ....23 H2
Arley La *NUNW/HART* CV10 ....22 B5
Arlington Wy *NUN* CV11 ....26 A5
Arlon Av *NUNW/HART* CV10 ....14 A5
Armadale Cl *HINC* LE10 ....17 H3
Armour Cl *HINC* LE10 ....28 C2
Armson Rd *RCOVN/BALC/EX* CV7 ....41 E4
Arncliffe Cl *NUN* CV11 ....26 B5
Arnold Rd
MKTBOS/BARL/STKG CV13 ....7 E3
Arran Cl *NUNW/HART* CV10 ....24 C4
Arran Wy *HINC* LE10 ....18 A3
Artillery Rd *NUN* CV11 ....38 C4
Arundel Rd *BDWTH* CV12 ....43 E2
Ascot Cl *BDWTH* CV12 ....41 F1
Ashbrook Ri *NUNW/HART* CV10 ....13 G2
Ashburton Cl *HINC* LE10 ....29 F1
Ashby Ct *NUN* CV11 ....25 G5
Ashby Gra *HINC* LE10 ....8 C4
Ashby Rd *HINC* LE10 ....8 D5
Ashdown Dr *NUNW/HART* CV10 ....24 C5
Ash Dr *NUNW/HART* CV10 ....13 F4
Ashe Rd *NUNW/HART* CV10 ....23 G4
Ashford Dr *BDWTH* CV12 ....41 E2
Ashford Rd *HINC* LE10 ....18 A5
Ash Green La
RCOVN/BALC/EX CV7 ....44 A2
Ash Gv *RCOVN/BALC/EX* CV7 ....44 A1
Ashington Rd *BDWTH* CV12 ....40 A4
Ashleigh Dr *NUN* CV11 ....37 F1
Ashleigh Gdns *RLEIW/BAR* LE9 ....9 H1
Ashridge Cl *NUN* CV11 ....37 F2
Ash Rd *RLEIW/BAR* LE9 ....10 A3
Ashurst Cl *COVN* CV6 ....45 F3
Ashwood Rd *NUNW/HART* CV10 ....24 B1
Aspen Dr *COVN* CV6 ....45 G2
Aster Cl *HINC* LE10 ....28 D1
NUN CV11 ....37 G1
Aster Wy *HINC* LE10 ....28 C2
Astley La *NUNW/HART* CV10 ....34 B4
Astley Rd *RLEIW/BAR* LE9 ....10 C3
Aston Flamville Rd *HINC* LE10 ....19 H5
Aston La *HINC* LE10 ....29 F1
HINC LE10 ....31 E3
Aston Rd *NUN* CV11 ....25 E2
Atherstone Rd *ATHST* CV9 ....3 F1
MKTBOS/BARL/STKG CV13 ....4 D2
NUNW/HART CV10 ....13 G2
Atholl Crs *NUNW/HART* CV10 ....24 B5
Atkins Wy *HINC* LE10 ....18 D5
Atterton La *ATHST* CV9 ....3 G3
Attleborough Rd *NUN* CV11 ....25 G5
Auden Cl *NUNW/HART* CV10 ....23 E3
Aulton Crs *HINC* LE10 ....18 A3
Aulton Wy *HINC* LE10 ....18 A3
Austen Cl *NUNW/HART* CV10 ....23 E2
Austin Cl *ATHST* CV9 ....2 C4
Avebury Cl *NUN* CV11 ....26 A5
Avenue North *RLEIW/BAR* LE9 ....10 D1
Avenue Rd *NUN* CV11 ....25 G5
Avenue South *RLEIW/BAR* LE9 ....10 D2
Aviemore Cl *NUNW/HART* CV10 ....24 D5
Avon Cl *BDWTH* CV12 ....37 H4
Axminster Cl *NUN* CV11 ....25 H2
Ayrshire Cl *RLEIW/BAR* LE9 ....9 F3
Aysgarth Cl *NUN* CV11 ....26 B5
Azalea Cl *HINC* LE10 ....28 C2
Azalea Dr *HINC* LE10 ....28 D1

B

Bachelors Bench *ATHST* CV9 ....2 C4
Back St *NUN* CV11 ....25 F2
Baker St *COVN* CV6 ....45 F2
Balfour Cl *HINC* LE10 ....18 D5
Balliol Rd *HINC* LE10 ....29 E1
Balmoral Rd *RLEIW/BAR* LE9 ....10 A3
Bank Rd *ATHST* CV9 ....2 D3
Bank Ter *RLEIW/BAR* LE9 ....9 F3
Banky Meadow *HINC* LE10 ....19 F5
Barbridge Cl *BDWTH* CV12 ....43 E3
Barbridge Rd *BDWTH* CV12 ....42 D3
Bardon Rd *RLEIW/BAR* LE9 ....9 G1
Bardsey Cl *HINC* LE10 ....18 A3
Barleston Dr *HINC* LE10 ....17 H3
Barleyfield *HINC* LE10 ....18 B1
Barling Wy *NUNW/HART* CV10 ....36 B1
Barlow Rd *COVE* CV2 ....45 H5
Barnacle La *BDWTH* CV12 ....43 E4
Barne Cl *NUN* CV11 ....37 H3
Barnsley Cl *ATHST* CV9 ....2 C4
Barons Cft *NUNW/HART* CV10 ....23 H3
Barpool Rd *NUNW/HART* CV10 ....24 C3
The Barracks *RLEIW/BAR* LE9 ....9 F3
Barrie Rd *HINC* LE10 ....18 C1
Barr La
MKTBOS/BARL/STKG CV13 ....16 C1
Barsby Cl *ATHST* CV9 ....2 C4
Barston Cl *COVN* CV6 ....45 E5
Barton Rd *BDWTH* CV12 ....41 F1
NUNW/HART CV10 ....36 C1
Barwell La *HINC* LE10 ....18 D1
Basford Brook Dr *COVN* CV6 ....44 D3
Basin Br
MKTBOS/BARL/STKG CV13 ....6 D4
Basin Bridge La
MKTBOS/BARL/STKG CV13 ....7 E5
Basley Wy *COVN* CV6 ....44 B4
Bassett La *RLEIW/BAR* LE9 ....31 G1
Bath Cl *RLEIW/BAR* LE9 ....21 G5
Bath Rd *ATHST* CV9 ....2 D4
NUN CV11 ....25 F2
Battledown Cl *HINC* LE10 ....18 A2
Bayliss Av *COVN* CV6 ....45 E4
Bayton Rd *RCOVN/BALC/EX* CV7 ....45 E1
Bayton Wy *RCOVN/BALC/EX* CV7 ....45 G1
Bazzard Rd *NUN* CV11 ....38 D4
Beacon Rd *COVN* CV6 ....44 B5
Bearsdon Crs *HINC* LE10 ....18 A3
Beattie Cl *HINC* LE10 ....18 C1
Beaufort Cl *HINC* LE10 ....28 C3
Beaumont Av *HINC* LE10 ....17 H5
Beaumont Pl *NUNW/HART* CV10 ....24 C3
Beaumont Rd *NUN* CV11 ....24 C3
Bedale Av *HINC* LE10 ....19 E2
Bede Rd *BDWTH* CV12 ....41 E1
NUNW/HART CV10 ....24 A3
Bede Village *BDWTH* CV12 * 40 A5
Bedford Cl *HINC* LE10 ....18 D1
Bedworth Cl *BDWTH* CV12 ....42 D3
Bedworth La *BDWTH* CV12 ....40 A1
Bedworth Rd *BDWTH* CV12 ....42 C3
COVN CV6 ....45 E3
Beech Cl *NUNW/HART* CV10 ....13 F4
Beechcroft *BDWTH* CV12 ....40 D4
The Beeches *BDWTH* CV12 ....40 C3
RLEIW/BAR LE9 ....10 C1
Beechwood Av *HINC* LE10 ....28 C4
Beechwood Rd *BDWTH* CV12 ....41 G1
NUNW/HART CV10 ....24 A1
Begonia Cl *HINC* LE10 ....28 D2
Begonia Dr *HINC* LE10 ....28 D1
Belfry Cl *HINC* LE10 ....28 C3
Bellairs Av *BDWTH* CV12 ....40 C4
Bell Dr *RCOVN/BALC/EX* CV7 ....44 C1
Belle Vue *NUNW/HART* CV10 * 24 B4
Belle Vue Rd *RLEIW/BAR* LE9 ....9 H1
Benbow Cl *HINC* LE10 ....8 C5
Bennet Cl
MKTBOS/BARL/STKG CV13 ....7 E3
Benn Rd *BDWTH* CV12 ....42 D3
Bentley Ct *COVN* CV6 ....44 A4
Bentley Rd *NUN* CV11 ....24 D3
RCOVN/BALC/EX CV7 ....41 E4
Berkeley Cl *NUNW/HART* CV10 ....24 D4
Berkshire Cl *NUNW/HART* CV10 ....24 B4
Bermuda Pk *NUNW/HART* CV10 ....36 A4
Bermuda Rd *NUNW/HART* CV10 ....36 A2
Berrington Rd
NUNW/HART CV10 ....14 A5
Berwyn Wy *NUNW/HART* CV10 ....23 H3
Beryl Av *HINC* LE10 ....17 H2
Bettina Cl *NUNW/HART* CV10 ....23 G2
Beverley Av *NUNW/HART* CV10 ....23 G3
Billington Rd East
RLEIW/BAR LE9 ....20 B1
Billington Rd West
RLEIW/BAR LE9 ....10 A5
Birch Cl *BDWTH* CV12 ....41 H1
RLEIW/BAR LE9 ....10 A4
The Birches *BDWTH* CV12 ....42 D1
Birchtree Rd *NUNW/HART* CV10 ....23 H1
Birkdale Cl *NUN* CV11 ....37 G1
Black-a-Tree Ct
NUNW/HART CV10 * 24 C2
Black-a-Tree Pl
NUNW/HART CV10 * 24 B3
Black-a-Tree Rd
NUNW/HART CV10 ....24 B3
Black Bank *RCOVN/BALC/EX* CV7 ....41 F4
Blackberry La
RCOVN/BALC/EX CV7 ....44 A3
Blackburn Rd *COVN* CV6 ....44 D5
RLEIW/BAR LE9 ....9 F3
Black Horse Rd *COVN* CV6 ....45 F3
Blackthorn Gv *NUN* CV11 ....26 A5
Bladon Cl *NUN* CV11 ....16 A4
Blair Dr *BDWTH* CV12 ....40 B4
Blake Cl *HINC* LE10 ....8 C5
NUNW/HART CV10 ....23 F2
Blenheim Av *COVN* CV6 ....44 A5
Blenheim Cl *HINC* LE10 ....19 E1
NUN CV11 ....26 A5
Blockley Rd *BDWTH* CV12 ....41 G1
Bluebell Dr *BDWTH* CV12 ....40 C3
Blyth Cl *BDWTH* CV12 ....40 A4
Bond Ga *NUN* CV11 ....25 F3
Bond Gate Chambers
NUN CV11 * 25 F3
Bond St *NUN* CV11 ....25 F2
Bonington Dr *BDWTH* CV12 ....41 E1
The Borough *HINC* LE10 ....18 C4
Borrowdale Cl *RLEIW/BAR* LE9 ....10 C3
Bostock Cl *RLEIW/BAR* LE9 ....20 C1
Boston Wy *RLEIW/BAR* LE9 ....9 E3
Bosworth Cl *HINC* LE10 ....17 H4
Bosworth Gn *RLEIW/BAR* LE9 ....11 E1
Bottrill St *NUN* CV11 ....25 E2
Bournebrook Vw
RCOVN/BALC/EX CV7 ....32 C1
Bourne Cl *ATHST* CV9 ....2 D1
Bowling Green La
RCOVN/BALC/EX CV7 ....44 C1
Bowling Green Rd *HINC* LE10 ....18 D3
Bowman Gn *HINC* LE10 ....29 E1
Boyslade Rd *HINC* LE10 ....28 D1
Boyslade Rd East *HINC* LE10 ....29 E2
Bracebridge Rd *ATHST* CV9 ....2 B4
Bracebridge St *NUN* CV11 ....25 E3
Brackendale Dr
NUNW/HART CV10 ....24 C4
Bradestone Rd *NUN* CV11 ....36 D2
Bradgate Rd *HINC* LE10 ....19 E2
RLEIW/BAR LE9 ....9 G1
Brading Rd *NUNW/HART* CV10 ....25 G1
Braemar Wy *NUNW/HART* CV10 ....24 D5
Bramble Cl *NUN* CV11 ....26 A5
Bramcote Cl *BDWTH* CV12 ....43 F3
HINC LE10 ....19 E1
Bramdene Av *NUNW/HART* CV10 ....15 F4
Brame Rd *HINC* LE10 ....18 B2
Brampton Wy *BDWTH* CV12 ....42 D2
Bramwell Gdns
RCOVN/BALC/EX CV7 ....44 D3
Brandon Rd *HINC* LE10 ....18 A5
Bransdale Av *COVN* CV6 ....44 B5
Brascote Rd *HINC* LE10 ....17 G4
Breach La *RLEIW/BAR* LE9 ....10 C4
Brechin Cl *HINC* LE10 ....17 H4
Brendon Wy *NUNW/HART* CV10 ....23 F4
Brenfield Dr *HINC* LE10 ....17 H4
Bretts Hall Est *NUNW/HART* CV10 ....13 E5
Brewer Rd *BDWTH* CV12 ....43 F4
Briansway *COVN* CV6 ....44 C5
Briar Cl *HINC* LE10 ....29 E1
Briardene Av *BDWTH* CV12 ....41 F4
Briarmead *HINC* LE10 ....28 D3
Briars Cl *NUN* CV11 ....25 H2

Brick Kiln St *HINC* LE10.....18 B4
Bridge La *ATHST* CV9.....3 F4
Bridge Rd *HINC* LE10.....18 C5
Bridge St *NUN* CV11.....25 F5
Bridle Path Rd *RLEIW/BAR* LE9.....20 A1
Brindley Cl *ATHST* CV9.....2 B1
Brindley Rd *HINC* LE10.....17 F4
  RCOVN/BALC/EX CV7.....45 F1
Briscoe Rd *COVN* CV6.....44 A4
Britannia Rd *HINC* LE10.....29 F2
Britten Cl *NUN* CV11.....37 G3
Brixham Cl *NUN* CV11.....26 A2
Broadsword Wy *HINC* LE10.....28 C3
Brockenhurst Wy *COVN* CV6.....45 F2
Brockey Cl *RLEIW/BAR* LE9.....9 G2
Brockhurst Av *HINC* LE10.....28 C3
Brodick Cl *HINC* LE10.....17 H4
Brodick Rd *HINC* LE10.....17 G4
Brodick Wy *NUNW/HART* CV10.....24 C4
Bronte Cl *NUNW/HART* CV10.....23 F3
Bronze Cl *NUN* CV11.....37 G2
Brookdale *HINC* LE10.....18 A4
Brookdale Rd *NUNW/HART* CV10 .15 G5
Brookfield *HINC* LE10.....31 F3
Brookfield Rd *HINC* LE10.....28 B1
Brook La *HINC* CV10.....25 F1
Brooklea *BDWTH* CV12.....40 D3
Brookside *HINC* LE10.....18 C5
Brook St *BDWTH* CV12.....36 B5
Brook Wk *ATHST* CV9.....3 E5
Broomfield Rd *NUNW/HART* CV10 .24 A3
Brosdale Dr *HINC* LE10.....17 H3
Broughton Rd *RLEIW/BAR* LE9.....21 H3
Browning Cl *NUNW/HART* CV10 ...23 F2
Browning Dr *HINC* LE10.....18 B3
Brown's Cl *RLEIW/BAR* LE9.....21 H5
Bruce Rd *RCOVN/BALC/EX* CV7.....44 D1
Brunel Rd *HINC* LE10.....18 B1
Bryant Rd *RCOVN/BALC/EX* CV7.....45 E1
Bryony Cl *BDWTH* CV12.....40 C4
Buchan Cl *NUNW/HART* CV10.....23 E3
Buckingham Cl *HINC* LE10.....9 E5
  NUNW/HART CV10.....36 B1
Buckingham's Wy *HINC* LE10.....31 E4
Bucks Hl *NUNW/HART* CV10.....13 G5
Buckwell Rd *RLEIW/BAR* LE9.....21 G5
Bulkington La *NUN* CV11.....37 G2
Bulkington Rd *BDWTH* CV12.....41 H3
  BDWTH CV12.....43 F5
Bullfurlong La *HINC* LE10.....29 E3
Bull Ring *HINC* LE10.....25 E5
Bull St *NUN* CV11.....25 C5
Bungalow Est *COVN* CV6 *.....44 D4
Burbage Common Rd
  RLEIW/BAR LE9.....19 G1
Burbage Rd *HINC* LE10.....19 F4
Burbages La *COVN* CV6.....44 B3
Burbury Cl *BDWTH* CV12.....41 C1
Burgage Pl *NUN* CV11.....25 F3
Burghley Cl *NUN* CV11.....26 A5
Burleigh Rd *HINC* LE10.....18 C3
Burlington Rd *NUNW/HART* CV10..36 B3
Burnaby Cl *NUNW/HART* CV10.....23 G2
Burnham Ri *NUN* CV11.....26 B1
Burns Wk *BDWTH* CV12.....41 G4
Burton La *NUN* CV11.....38 D3
Bute Cl *HINC* LE10.....18 B3
Butlers Crs *RCOVN/BALC/EX* CV7...41 F4
Butlin Rd *COVN* CV6.....44 A4
Buttermere Av *NUN* CV11.....26 B1
Butt La *HINC* LE10.....18 D3
Butt Lane Cl *HINC* LE10.....18 D3
Byford St *NUNW/HART* CV10.....24 C3
Byron Av *BDWTH* CV12.....41 H3
Byron St *RLEIW/BAR* LE9.....9 G1
  RLEIW/BAR LE9.....10 B3

C

Cadeby Cl *HINC* LE10.....18 A2
Cadles Cl *RLEIW/BAR* LE9.....21 G2
Cadman Cl *BDWTH* CV12.....41 G2
Caernarfon Dr *NUN* CV11.....25 C4
Caldecote Cl *NUNW/HART* CV10 ...15 F4
Calder Cl *BDWTH* CV12.....42 D3
Caldon Cl *HINC* LE10.....18 A4
Caldwell Rd *NUN* CV11.....36 D1
Callendar Cl *NUN* CV11.....16 B5
Calvert Crs *RLEIW/BAR* LE9.....31 H1
Camborne Dr *NUN* CV11.....26 A2
Cambourne Rd *HINC* LE10.....29 F1
Cambridge Dr *NUNW/HART* CV10 ..24 A4
Campbell Cl *NUNW/HART* CV10.....23 F3
Camp Hill Dr *NUNW/HART* CV10 ...24 A1

Camp Hill Rd *NUNW/HART* CV10 ....13 H5
Campling Cl *BDWTH* CV12.....42 D3
Campton Cl *HINC* LE10.....18 D5
Canalside *COVN* CV6.....45 F2
Canal Wy *HINC* LE10.....17 G5
Canberra Rd *COVE* CV2.....45 G4
Canberra Wy *HINC* LE10.....28 D3
Candle La *RLEIW/BAR* LE9.....10 C2
Canning St *HINC* LE10.....18 B3
Canon Dr *RCOVN/BALC/EX* CV7 ...44 B2
Canterbury Wy *NUN* CV11.....16 B4
Cardigan Rd *BDWTH* CV12.....40 A4
Carey Hill Rd *RLEIW/BAR* LE9.....21 G3
Cargill Cl *COVN* CV6.....44 D3
Carisbrook Rd *NUNW/HART* CV10...25 G1
Carlton Cl *BDWTH* CV12.....42 D2
Carlyle Cl *NUNW/HART* CV10.....23 E2
Carlyon Rd *ATHST* CV9.....2 D2
Carnoustie Cl *NUN* CV11.....38 A2
Caroline Cl *NUN* CV11.....37 F3
Carpenters Cl *HINC* LE10.....29 E2
Carr's Dr *RLEIW/BAR* LE9.....10 C2
Carrs Hl *RLEIW/BAR* LE9.....9 H3
Carr's Rd *RLEIW/BAR* LE9.....10 C2
Carsal Cl *RCOVN/BALC/EX* CV7...44 B3
Cashmore Rd *BDWTH* CV12.....40 C4
Castle Cl *HINC* LE10.....31 G1
Castle Ct *HINC* LE10.....28 C1
Castle Dr *NUNW/HART* CV10.....34 A3
Castlemaine Dr *HINC* LE10.....18 D1
Castle Rd *NUNW/HART* CV10.....13 G3
  NUNW/HART CV10.....15 F5
Castle St *HINC* LE10.....18 C5
Castle Vw *NUNW/HART* CV10.....13 G3
Cavalier Cl *NUN* CV11.....37 E1
Caversham Cl *NUN* CV11.....16 A5
Cecil Leonard Knox Crs
  NUN CV11.....38 D4
Cedar Rd *NUNW/HART* CV10.....24 A1
Cedars Av *HINC* LE10.....10 A3
Cedars Rd *RCOVN/BALC/EX* CV7 ...41 F4
Celandine Wy *BDWTH* CV12.....40 C3
Cemetery La *NUNW/HART* CV10 ...13 G3
Centenary Wy *NUNW/HART* CV10..36 H1
Central Av *NUN* CV11.....25 E2
Chalfont Cl *BDWTH* CV12.....41 E1
Chamberlaine St *BDWTH* CV12.....41 F1
Chancery La *NUNW/HART* CV10 ...13 G5
Chandos St *NUN* CV11.....24 D3
Change Brook Cl *NUN* CV11.....16 A4
Chapel La *ATHST* CV9.....3 H3
  HINC LE10.....31 F4
Chapel St *BDWTH* CV12.....41 F2
  HINC LE10.....31 F4
  NUN CV11.....25 F3
  RLEIW/BAR LE9.....9 F3
  RLEIW/BAR LE9.....10 D1
Chapel Yd *COVE* CV2 *.....45 H3
Charlecote Wk *NUN* CV11.....37 F2
Charles Eaton Rd *BDWTH* CV12...40 D2
Charles Rd *ATHST* CV9.....3 E4
Charles St *HINC* LE10.....18 C3
  NUN CV11.....24 D2
  RCOVN/BALC/EX CV7.....33 E2
Charleston Crs *RLEIW/BAR* LE9 ....9 F3
Charnwood Av
  NUNW/HART CV10.....24 B1
Charnwood Cl *HINC* LE10.....18 D2
Charnwood Dr
  NUNW/HART CV10.....13 F2
Charnwood Rd *HINC* LE10.....18 C3
  RLEIW/BAR LE9.....9 G1
Chartwell Cl *NUN* CV11.....37 F1
Chase Cl *NUNW/HART* CV10.....23 G5
Chatsworth Dr *NUN* CV11.....26 A5
Chaucer Dr *HINC* LE10.....18 A3
Cheadle Cl *COVN* CV6.....45 E4
Chelsea Cl *NUN* CV11.....16 A5
Cheltenham Cl *BDWTH* CV12.....41 F1
Chequer St *BDWTH* CV12.....42 A3
Cherryfield Cl *NUNW/HART* CV10 .13 G2
Cherry Tree Av
  NUNW/HART CV10.....24 B1
Cherry Tree Dr *RLEIW/BAR* LE9 ....9 G1
Cherwell Cl *HINC* LE10.....17 H4
Chessher St *HINC* LE10.....18 B3
Chesterfield Wy *RLEIW/BAR* LE9...9 H2
Chesterton Dr *NUNW/HART* CV10..23 E3
Chestnut Crs *NUNW/HART* CV10 ..24 B2
Chestnut Rd *BDWTH* CV12.....41 H1
The Chestnuts *BDWTH* CV12.....40 C3
Chetwynd Dr *NUN* CV11.....37 H3
Cheveral Av *BDWTH* CV12.....41 E2
Cheverel Pl *NUN* CV11.....25 E4
Cheverel St *NUN* CV11.....25 E4
Cheviot Cl *NUNW/HART* CV10.....23 G4
Chichester Cl *NUN* CV11.....16 B5
Chilworth Cl *NUN* CV11.....37 E2
The Chines *NUNW/HART* CV10 *...15 G5

Chingford Rd *COVN* CV6.....45 E4
Choyce Cl *ATHST* CV9.....2 C1
Christchurch Cl
  NUNW/HART CV10.....35 H1
Church Cl
  MKTBOS/BARL/STKG CV13.....7 E2
  NUNW/HART CV10.....13 G4
  RLEIW/BAR LE9.....9 F3
Churchdale Cl *NUNW/HART* CV10 .23 H3
Church La
  MKTBOS/BARL/STKG CV13.....4 C3
  NUNW/HART CV10.....15 F5
  NUNW/HART CV10.....33 H1
  RCOVN/BALC/EX CV7.....44 C1
  RLEIW/BAR LE9.....9 F3
Church Rd *ATHST* CV9.....3 G4
  BDWTH CV12.....43 E3
  HINC LE10.....29 F1
  NUN CV11.....25 G3
  RLEIW/BAR LE9.....9 F3
  RLEIW/BAR LE9.....21 G3
  RLEIW/BAR LE9.....31 G1
Church St *ATHST* CV9.....2 D4
  BDWTH CV12.....43 E3
  HINC LE10.....18 D4
  NUN CV11.....25 G3
  RLEIW/BAR LE9.....9 F3
  RLEIW/BAR LE9.....21 G3
  RLEIW/BAR LE9.....31 G1
Church Wk *ATHST* CV9.....3 E4
  HINC LE10.....18 C4
Church Wks
  MKTBOS/BARL/STKG CV13.....7 E2
Church Wy *BDWTH* CV12.....41 F2
Cicey La *NUN* CV11.....39 E2
The Circle *NUNW/HART* CV10.....24 B3
Claremont Cl *BDWTH* CV12.....42 D1
Clarence Rd *HINC* LE10.....18 D4
Clarence St *NUN* CV11.....25 E4
Clarendon Rd *HINC* LE10.....18 B5
Clay Av *NUN* CV11.....16 A5
Clear View Crs *RLEIW/BAR* LE9 ....10 C1
Clement St *NUN* CV11.....25 E4
Clent Dr *NUNW/HART* CV10.....23 G4
Cleveland Rd *BDWTH* CV12.....42 D2
  HINC LE10.....18 B4
Cleveley Dr *NUNW/HART* CV10.....14 A5
Clifton Rd *NUNW/HART* CV10.....24 D3
Clifton Wy *HINC* LE10.....17 H3
Clinic Dr *NUN* CV11.....25 F4
Clint Hill Dr *RLEIW/BAR* LE9.....21 H3
Cliveden Wk *NUN* CV11.....37 G2
Clivesway *HINC* LE10.....18 B2
The Cloisters *RLEIW/BAR* LE9.....10 B2
The Close *RLEIW/BAR* LE9.....9 F2
Clovelly Wy *NUN* CV11.....25 H2
Cloverfield *HINC* LE10.....18 B1
Clover Pk *HINC* LE10.....18 A1
Clunes Av *NUN* CV11.....25 H1
Clyde Rd *BDWTH* CV12.....42 C2
Coalpit Fields Rd *BDWTH* CV12 ...41 G3
Colbek Ct *NUNW/HART* CV10.....22 D3
Coldstream Cl *HINC* LE10.....17 H3
Coleshill Rd *ATHST* CV9.....2 B5
  NUNW/HART CV10.....12 C4
Coley Cl *HINC* LE10.....18 C5
College La *HINC* LE10.....18 D3
College St *NUNW/HART* CV10.....25 F5
Colliers Wy *NUNW/HART* CV10.....24 C3
Colliery La *RCOVN/BALC/EX* CV7 ..41 F4
Colts Cl *HINC* LE10.....28 C3
Columbia Gdns *BDWTH* CV12.....41 H3
Columbine Wy *BDWTH* CV12.....40 C4
The Common *RLEIW/BAR* LE9.....9 G3
Conifer Cl *BDWTH* CV12.....41 G1
Coniston Cl *BDWTH* CV12.....43 E2
  RLEIW/BAR LE9.....10 C2
Coniston Wy *NUN* CV11.....16 A5
Constable Cl *BDWTH* CV12.....36 A5
Constance Cl
  RCOVN/BALC/EX CV7.....40 D5
Convent Cl *ATHST* CV9.....3 E4
Convent La *ATHST* CV9.....2 D4
Conwy Cl *NUN* CV11.....25 C4
Cook Cl *COVN* CV6.....45 E4
Cooks Cl *ATHST* CV9.....2 C3
Cook's La *RLEIW/BAR* LE9.....31 G1
Co-operative St *COVE* CV2.....45 F5
Cooper St *NUN* CV11.....25 G3
Cope Arnolds Cl *COVN* CV6 *.....44 D3
Coppice Cl *HINC* LE10.....19 E1
The Coppice *ATHST* CV9.....19 E4
  HINC LE10.....19 E4
  NUNW/HART CV10.....25 F5
The Copse *RCOVN/BALC/EX* CV7 ..41 E5
Copsewood Av *NUN* CV11.....37 H3
Coral Cl *HINC* LE10.....29 E3
Corley Vw *RCOVN/BALC/EX* CV7 ..44 A1
Cornfield *HINC* LE10.....8 B5
Cornish Cl *NUNW/HART* CV10.....13 G4
Cornish Crs *NUNW/HART* CV10 ...24 D5
Corn Mdw *BDWTH* CV12.....41 G3
Cornwall Wy *HINC* LE10.....8 D5

Coronation Rd *RLEIW/BAR* LE9 10
Coronel Av *COVN* CV6.....44
Corporation St *NUN* CV11.....25
Cotes Rd *HINC* LE10.....29
Cotman Cl *BDWTH* CV12.....41
Cotman Dr *HINC* LE10.....17
Coton Rd *NUN* CV11.....25
Cotswold Crs *NUNW/HART* CV10...23
Cottage Gdns *RLEIW/BAR* LE9 10
Cotton Arches Rbt *NUN* CV11.....25
Council Rd *HINC* LE10.....18
Countess Rd *NUN* CV11.....24
Courtney Cl *HINC* LE10.....16
Coventry Rd *BDWTH* CV12.....41
  BDWTH CV12.....42
  HINC LE10.....18
  LUTT LE17.....31
  NUNW/HART CV10.....10
Coventry Rd Exhall
  RCOVN/BALC/EX CV7.....45
Coventry St *NUN* CV11.....25
Coventry Wy *BDWTH* CV12.....40
Cowper Rd *HINC* LE10.....25
Cox's Cl *NUNW/HART* CV10.....25
Cozens Cl *BDWTH* CV12.....41
Crabtree Rd *RLEIW/BAR* LE9 9
Craddock Dr *NUNW/HART* CV10 ...13
Crammond Cl *HINC* LE10.....18
Crantock Wy *NUN* CV11.....26
Crediton Cl *NUN* CV11.....26
The Crescent *RLEIW/BAR* LE9 10
Cresswell Cl *NUNW/HART* CV10 ...15
Croft Cl *RLEIW/BAR* LE9.....9
Croft Flds *BDWTH* CV12.....41
Croft Md *NUNW/HART* CV10.....22
Croft Pool *BDWTH* CV12.....40
Croft Rd *ATHST* CV9.....2
  BDWTH CV12.....40
  NUNW/HART CV10.....24
The Croft *BDWTH* CV12.....42
  COVN CV6.....44
Cromarty Dr *HINC* LE10.....17
Cromdale Cl *NUNW/HART* CV10 ...23
Crondal Rd *RCOVN/BALC/EX* CV7 ..45
Crosskirk Rd *HINC* LE10.....17
Crossland Rw *HINC* LE10.....29
Cross St *NUNW/HART* CV10.....24
Crossways *HINC* LE10.....29
Crowhill Rd *NUN* CV11.....26
Crownhill Rd *HINC* LE10.....29
Croxhall St *BDWTH* CV12.....41
Crummock Cl *COVN* CV6.....44
Cubbington Rd *COVN* CV6.....45
Culpepper Cl *NUNW/HART* CV10 ..24
Cumberland Dr
  NUNW/HART CV10.....24
Cumberland Wy *RLEIW/BAR* LE9...9
Cumbrae Dr *HINC* LE10.....18

D

Daffern Av *RCOVN/BALC/EX* CV7...7
Daffern Rd *RCOVN/BALC/EX* CV7 ..44
Dahlia Cl *HINC* LE10.....28
Dale End *NUNW/HART* CV10.....24
Dale End Cl *HINC* LE10.....17
Dalmahoy Cl *NUN* CV11.....38
Dalton Rd *BDWTH* CV12.....40
Daniel Av *NUNW/HART* CV10.....23
Daniel Rd *ATHST* CV9.....3
Dare's Wk *HINC* LE10.....18
Dark La *BDWTH* CV12.....28
Darley Rd *HINC* LE10.....28
Dart Cl *HINC* LE10.....18
Dartington Wy *NUN* CV11.....37
Darwin Cl *HINC* LE10.....18
Davenport Ter *HINC* LE10.....18
David Rd *RCOVN/BALC/EX* CV7 44
Davies Rd *RCOVN/BALC/EX* CV7 ...45
Dawlish Cl *NUN* CV11.....25
Dawson's La *RLEIW/BAR* LE9.....9
Deacon St *NUN* CV11.....25
Dean Cl *HINC* LE10.....18
Dean Rd *HINC* LE10.....18
Dean Rd West *HINC* LE10.....18
Deans Wy *RCOVN/BALC/EX* CV7...44
Dehaviland Cl *NUN* CV11.....25
De-la-Bere Crs *HINC* LE10.....29
Delage Cl *COVN* CV6.....45
Delamere Rd *BDWTH* CV12.....40
De Montfort Rd *HINC* LE10.....4
Dempster Rd *BDWTH* CV12.....4
Denehurst Wy *NUNW/HART* CV10..23
Denham Ct *ATHST* CV9.....9

...nis Rd HINC LE10 ....28 B2
...rby Rd HINC LE10 ....18 C2
...ronda CI BDWTH CV12 ....41 E2
...rwent CI RLEIW/BAR LE9 ....10 C3
...rwent Rd BDWTH CV12 ....41 E3
...rwent Wy NUN CV11 ....26 A1
...veron Wy HINC LE10 ....18 A3
...von CI NUNW/HART CV10.........24 C4
...voran CI RCOVN/BALC/EX CV7 ..41 F5
...kens CI NUNW/HART CV10 ....23 F3
...sbury Rd
RCOVN/BALC/EX CV7 ....41 E4
...am CI COVN CV6 ....45 E4
...e Dingle NUNW/HART CV10 ....24 B1
...gley Rd BDWTH CV12 ....42 D3
...ney CI RLEIW/BAR LE9 ....21 G3
...ctor Cookes CI RLEIW/BAR LE9....9 F3
...ctors Flds RLEIW/BAR LE9 ....10 A3
...dgson CI COVN CV6 ....45 E4
...dwells Rd HINC LE10 ....17 F4
...nnithorne Av
NUNW/HART CV10 ....36 C1
...rcas CI NUN CV11 ....37 H2
...rchester Rd HINC LE10 ....19 G5
...rchester Wy NUN CV11 ....16 B5
...lecote Rd NUNW/HART CV10...36 D2
...lecote PI NUNW/HART CV10 ......36 C2
...wning Crs BDWTH CV12 ....41 G1
...le Dr COVN CV6 ....44 D5
...ke Wy HINC LE10 ....8 C5
...yton CI
MKTBOS/BARL/STKG CV13 ......4 B3
...UNW/HART CV10 ....36 C1
...yton Ct NUNW/HART CV10 *.....13 G2
...yton La
MKTBOS/BARL/STKG CV13 ......4 B3
...yton Rd BDWTH CV12 ....41 G3
...yton Wy NUNW/HART CV10.......13 H5
... Drive RLEIW/BAR LE9 ....9 G1
...ld St HINC LE10 ....18 C3
...den CI NUNW/HART CV10 ....23 E2
...ley Ri HINC LE10 ....28 C1
...ley St ATHST CV9 ....2 C4
...dale St NUN CV11 ....25 F3
...e St NUN CV11 ....24 D3
...blane Wy HINC LE10 ....17 H3
...ster PI COVN CV6 ....44 B5
...ort Rd HINC LE10 ....19 E5
...ton Rd COVE CV9 ....45 H5
...rs Rd NUN CV11 ....38 D4
...nond CI COVN CV6 ....44 A5

E

...ie St NUNW/HART CV10 ....23 H3
...e CI NUN CV11 ....37 H2
...Shilton Rd RLEIW/BAR LE9 ......11 F1
...s Rd NUN CV11 ....24 D2
...St BDWTH CV12 ....41 H3
...LEIW/BAR LE9 ....10 D1
...edale CI NUN CV11 ....26 B1
...t Av BDWTH CV12 ....41 H3
...tboro Wy NUN CV11 ....25 H5
...c CI HINC LE10 ....18 C5
... Equity Rd RLEIW/BAR LE9 ....10 C1
...field Rd NUNW/HART CV10.......25 G1
...Gn RLEIW/BAR LE9 ....9 F3
...woods Rd HINC LE10 ....19 E2
...rne Rd COVE CV2 ....45 C5
...e Miller Ct BDWTH CV12 *........40 A1
...dale Dr HINC LE10 ....18 D1
...burgh Rd NUNW/HART CV10 ....24 A4
...LEIW/BAR LE9 ....10 A3
...ard Rd BDWTH CV12 ....41 G3
...ard St HINC LE10 ....18 B2
...NUN CV11 ....25 E3
...ard Tyler Rd BDWTH CV12 ....41 E4
...wean-Walker Ct NUN CV11 * 25 F2
...r CI NUN CV11 ....37 G3
... Wy NUNW/HART CV10 ....36 B1
...beth Rd HINC LE10 ....18 C3
...man Gdns COVN CV6 ....44 D5
...mere Rd BDWTH CV12 ....41 H3
...on CI RLEIW/BAR LE9 ....21 G2
...dale Rd RLEIW/BAR LE9 ....10 A4
...esthorpe La RLEIW/BAR LE9 .....9 H2
...field Rd NUNW/HART CV10 ....15 F5

Elmhurst Rd COVN CV6...................45 E4
The Elms BDWTH CV12 ....40 C3
Elm Tree Dr HINC LE10 ....19 E4
Elm Tree Rd BDWTH CV12 ....43 F3
Elm Wy NUNW/HART CV10 ....13 F4
Elwy Cir RCOVN/BALC/EX CV7 ....44 A1
Embleton CI HINC LE10 ....18 A4
Ennerdale Crs NUN CV11 ....26 A1
Ensor CI NUN CV11 ....26 A1
Epsom CI BDWTH CV12 ....41 F1
Equity Rd RLEIW/BAR LE9 ....10 B3
Erdington Rd ATHST CV9 ....2 C4
Erica Av BDWTH CV12 ....40 C3
Ernest Richards Rd BDWTH CV12 ....41 F1
Erskine CI HINC LE10 ....17 H2
Eskdale Rd HINC LE10 ....17 H4
Eustace Rd BDWTH CV12 ....43 F4
Evans CI BDWTH CV12 ....41 G2
Exbury Wy NUN CV11 ....37 E2
Exhall Basin COVN CV6 * 45 F2
Exhall Gn RCOVN/BALC/EX CV7 ......44 D1
Exton CI RCOVN/BALC/EX CV7 ....44 A1

F

Factory Rd HINC LE10 ....18 C3
Fair Acre Rd RLEIW/BAR LE9 * 9 F3
Fairacre Rd RLEIW/BAR LE9 ....9 F3
Fair Isle Dr NUNW/HART CV10 ....24 C4
Fairway NUN CV11 ....37 H2
The Fairway HINC LE10 ....19 E5
Falcon CI NUN CV11 ....37 H2
Falconers Gn HINC LE10 ....29 E1
Fallowfields COVN CV6 ....44 A4
Falmouth CI NUN CV11 ....26 B2
Falmouth Dr HINC LE10 ....8 D5
Falstaff CI NUN CV11 ....37 G1
Faraday Rd HINC LE10 ....17 H5
Far Lash HINC LE10 ....19 E5
Farmcote Rd COVE CV2 ....45 H5
Farm Rd HINC LE10 ....28 D1
RLEIW/BAR LE9 ....9 H1
Farndale Av COVN CV6 ....44 B5
Farndon CI BDWTH CV12 ....42 D2
Farndon Dr RLEIW/BAR LE9 ....21 F3
Farneway HINC LE10 ....18 A3
Farriers Wy HINC LE10 ....29 E2
NUN CV11 ....26 A5
Faultlands CI NUN CV11 ....37 F2
Featherston Dr HINC LE10 ....18 C5
Featherstone CI
NUNW/HART CV10 ....25 F5
Featherston Rd HINC LE10 ....28 D1
Feilding Wy RLEIW/BAR LE9 ....23 F2
Fenn Lanes
MKTBOS/BARL/STKG CV13 ....5 H1
Ferndale CI NUN CV11 ....25 H2
Ferneley Av HINC LE10 ....17 H1
Ferness CI HINC LE10 ....18 A2
Ferness Rd HINC LE10 ....18 A2
Fern Gv BDWTH CV12 ....40 C4
Field CI HINC LE10 ....19 E1
Fielding CI ATHST CV9 ....2 C1
Field View CI
RCOVN/BALC/EX CV7 ....41 E5
Field Wy RLEIW/BAR LE9 ....10 A2
Fife St NUN CV11 ....24 D3
Fifield CI NUN CV11 ....25 G5
Findley CI ATHST CV9 ....3 E5
Findon CI BDWTH CV12 ....43 E2
Firleigh Dr BDWTH CV12 ....43 E2
The Firs BDWTH CV12 ....40 C3
Firtree CI BDWTH CV12 ....9 G1
Fir Tree Gv NUN CV11 ....36 D1
Firtree La RCOVN/BALC/EX CV7 ......33 E2
Fisher CI RLEIW/BAR LE9 ....21 F3
Fishers Wk ATHST CV9 * 2 D4
Fitton St NUN CV11 ....25 E4
Flamville Rd HINC LE10 ....29 G2
The Fleet HINC LE10 ....21 H2
Fleming Rd HINC LE10 ....17 F5
Fletcher Rd HINC LE10 ....18 D5
NUN CV11 ....21 H2
Flint CI ATHST CV9 ....2 D1
Florence CI HINC LE10 ....2 C2
RCOVN/BALC/EX CV7 ....40 D5
Florian Wy HINC LE10 ....17 H3
Flude Rd RCOVN/BALC/EX CV7 ......44 A1
Ford St NUNW/HART CV10 ....24 D3
Forest Rd HINC LE10 ....19 E4
Forest View Rd RLEIW/BAR LE9 ....9 H2
Forest Wy NUNW/HART CV10 ....24 B5
Forge Wy COVN CV6 ....44 A5
Forresters CI HINC LE10 ....29 E1

Forresters Rd HINC LE10 ....29 E1
Forryan Rd HINC LE10 ....19 E5
Fosse CI HINC LE10 ....31 E4
Fourfields Wy
RCOVN/BALC/EX CV7 ....32 D3
Fourways ATHST CV9 ....2 D3
Fox Av NUNW/HART CV10 ....15 F4
Foxcovert La
MKTBOS/BARL/STKG CV13 ....6 B1
Foxford Crs COVE CV2 ....45 F4
Foxglove CI NUN CV11 ....40 C4
Foxhills CI NUN CV11 ....38 A1
Fox Hollies HINC LE10 ....31 E4
Fox's Covert
MKTBOS/BARL/STKG CV13 ....4 C3
Frances Crs BDWTH CV12 ....41 E2
Frank Booton CI RLEIW/BAR LE9 ....11 E2
Franklin Rd NUN CV11 ....36 D1
Frank St NUN CV11 ....25 E4
Fraser CI NUNW/HART CV10 ....23 G1
Frederick Av HINC LE10 ....17 H2
Frederick Rd
RCOVN/BALC/EX CV7 ....32 D2
Freeman CI NUNW/HART CV10 ....24 A3
Freeman's La HINC LE10 ....25 H5
Freer St NUN CV11 ....25 H5
Freesland Ri NUNW/HART CV10 ....23 G1
Frensham Dr NUNW/HART CV10......23 G2
Freswick CI HINC LE10 ....17 G3
Frewen Dr RLEIW/BAR LE9 ....21 C5
Friar's Ga ATHST CV9 ....2 C3
Friary CI HINC LE10 ....18 D3
Friary Rd ATHST CV9 ....2 C2
Friary St NUN CV11 ....25 E2
Frisby Rd RLEIW/BAR LE9 ....9 G2
Friswell La RLEIW/BAR LE9 ....9 G2
Frith Wy HINC LE10 ....17 H1
Frobisher CI HINC LE10 ....8 C5
Furnace CI BDWTH CV12 ....41 G2
Furnace Rd BDWTH CV12 ....41 H2

G

Gadsby St NUN CV11 ....25 H4
Gainsborough Av HINC LE10 ....17 H1
Gainsborough Dr BDWTH CV12........41 F2
Gallagher Rd BDWTH CV12 ....41 E3
Galloway CI RLEIW/BAR LE9 ....9 E3
Gallus Dr HINC LE10 ....17 H3
Garden CI HINC LE10 ....28 C1
Garden Rd HINC LE10 ....18 B3
Garnette CI NUNW/HART CV10 ....23 G2
Garrett St NUN CV11 ....25 H5
Gartree Crs RLEIW/BAR LE9 ....10 A2
Gatehouse La BDWTH CV12 ....41 E3
George Eliot Av BDWTH CV12 ....41 H3
George Eliot St
NUNW/HART CV10 ....25 E5
George Foster CI RLEIW/BAR LE9 ...10 C1
George Fox La
MKTBOS/BARL/STKG CV13 ....4 C3
George Geary CI RLEIW/BAR LE9 ......9 H2
George Hill CI RLEIW/BAR LE9 ....21 G2
George Marriott CI
RLEIW/BAR LE9 ....21 F4
George St HINC LE10 ....18 C4
NUN CV11 ....25 C5
RCOVN/BALC/EX CV7 ....33 E2
RLEIW/BAR LE9 ....9 G2
George St Ringway BDWTH CV12.....41 H2
George Ward Ct RLEIW/BAR LE9 ......9 G2
Gibson Crs BDWTH CV12 ....41 E3
Gilfil Rd NUNW/HART CV10 ....36 B1
Gillet CI NUN CV11 ....25 E4
Gipsy La NUNW/HART CV10 ....24 B4
Girtin CI BDWTH CV12 ....41 E1
Gladstone CI HINC LE10 ....18 D1
Gladstone Ter HINC LE10 ....18 D4
Glaisdale Av COVN CV6 ....44 C5
Glebe Av BDWTH CV12 ....40 C4
Glebe La NUN CV11 ....26 A2
Glebe Rd HINC LE10 ....19 E4
NUN CV11 ....25 G3
Glen Bank HINC LE10 ....18 D3
Glenbarr CI HINC LE10 ....17 H4
Glenbarr Dr HINC LE10 ....17 H4
Glendon Gdns BDWTH CV12...........43 E2
Gleneagles CI HINC LE10 ....28 C3
NUN CV11 ....38 A2
Glenfield Av NUNW/HART CV10 ....15 F5
Glenmore Dr COVN CV6 ....44 D3
Glenmount Av COVN CV6 ....44 D3
Glenn St COVN CV6 ....44 B5
Glenridding CI COVN CV6 ....44 D3

Glenwood Gdns BDWTH CV12..........36 A5
Gloucester CI NUN CV11 ....16 B5
Glover's CI ATHST CV9 ....3 E4
Glyn CI RLEIW/BAR LE9 ....9 F2
Gold CI NUN CV11 ....37 E2
Golf Dr NUN CV11 ....37 H1
Goodyers End La
RCOVN/BALC/EX CV7 ....40 B5
Goosehills Rd HINC LE10 ....28 D2
Goose La RLEIW/BAR LE9 ....9 F4
Gopsall Rd HINC LE10 ....18 B2
Gordon CI BDWTH CV12 ....41 F1
Gorse Farm Rd NUN CV11 ....37 H2
Gorsy Wy NUNW/HART CV10 ....24 A2
Gosford Dr HINC LE10 ....17 H3
Gowrie CI HINC LE10 ....18 A2
Grace Rd RLEIW/BAR LE9 ....21 H5
Graham St NUN CV11 ....25 E2
Gramer Ct ATHST CV9 * 3 E5
Granby CI HINC LE10 ....18 B5
Granby Rd HINC LE10 ....18 B5
NUNW/HART CV10 ....24 C4
Grand Depot Rd NUN CV11 ....38 D4
Grange CI NUNW/HART CV10 ....13 H5
Grange Dr HINC LE10 ....28 D2
Grange Rd COVN CV6 ....45 F4
NUN CV11 ....13 G2
The Grange RLEIW/BAR LE9 ....10 B3
Grange Wk COVN CV6 * 45 F3
Grant Rd RCOVN/BALC/EX CV7 ......41 E5
Granville Gdns HINC LE10 ....18 B4
Granville Rd HINC LE10 ....18 B4
Grasmere Crs NUN CV11 ....16 A5
Grasmere Rd BDWTH CV12 ....41 E3
Grassington Dr NUN CV11 ....26 B5
Greendale CI ATHST CV9 ....2 D4
Greendale Rd ATHST CV9 ....2 D4
Greenhill Dr RLEIW/BAR LE9 ....9 G2
Greenhill Rd
MKTBOS/BARL/STKG CV13 ....7 E2
Green La NUNW/HART CV10...........13 H5
RLEIW/BAR LE9 ....10 B1
Greenmoor Rd HINC LE10...............28 B2
NUNW/HART CV10 ....24 D4
Greenodd Dr COVN CV6 ....44 D3
Greenside CI NUN CV11 ....37 H1
Greens Yd BDWTH CV12 * 41 G2
The Green NUN CV11 * 25 H5
Greenway NUN CV11 ....37 H1
Greenwood Rd
MKTBOS/BARL/STKG CV13 ....7 E2
Gresham Rd NUNW/HART CV10........36 B2
Griff La NUNW/HART CV10 ....35 E4
Grindle Rd COVN CV6 ....44 D4
Grosvenor Crs HINC LE10 ....29 F1
Grove Flds NUNW/HART CV10 ....15 F4
Grove Pk HINC LE10 ....29 F1
Grove PI NUNW/HART CV10 ....24 A4
Grove Rd ATHST CV9 ....2 C4
HINC LE10 ....29 E2
NUNW/HART CV10 ....24 A4
The Grove BDWTH CV12 ....41 F2
HINC LE10 ....18 B4
Gun HI RCOVN/BALC/EX CV7 ....33 G3
Gwendoline Av HINC LE10 ....17 H2
Gypsy La ATHST CV9 ....2 C1

H

Halberd CI HINC LE10 ....28 C2
Hall Dr MKTBOS/BARL/STKG CV13 ...7 F2
Hall End NUN CV11 ....25 G5
Hall Gdns ATHST CV9 * 3 F3
Hall La ATHST CV9 ....3 G3
Hall Rd HINC LE10 ....28 C1
Halls Crs HINC LE10 ....31 E4
Hamilton CI BDWTH CV12 ....40 A4
HINC LE10 ....17 H2
Hamlet CI NUN CV11 ....37 G1
Hammersley St BDWTH CV12 ....40 C4
Hammond CI NUN CV11 ....25 H4
Hampton Av NUNW/HART CV10 ....23 G3
Hanbury Rd BDWTH CV12 ....41 G1
Hangman's La HINC LE10 ....18 C1
Hansom Rd HINC LE10 ....19 E2
Hanson Wy COVN CV6.....................45 E4
Harcourt Gdns NUN CV11 ....25 F4
Hardy CI HINC LE10 ....8 C5
NUNW/HART CV10 ....23 F3
Hare & Hounds La
NUNW/HART CV10 ....24 D5
Harecroft Crs RLEIW/BAR LE9 ....21 H5
Harefield La NUNW/HART CV10........35 H2
Harefield Rd NUN CV11 ....25 F3

Harmony Ct NUNW/HART CV10......25 E5
Harold St NUN CV11......25 F4
Harpers La ATHST CV9......3 F5
Harrison Cl HINC LE10......10 C2
Harrison Crs BDWTH CV12......41 E3
Harrowbrook Rd HINC LE10....17 F5
Harrow Cl COVN CV6......45 E4
Harwood Dr HINC LE10......9 E5
Haselbury Cnr
 NUNW/HART CV10......35 H1
Hastings Dr RLEIW/BAR LE9......9 G2
Hathaway Dr NUN CV11......37 G1
Hatters Ct BDWTH CV12......41 G3
Hatters Dr ATHST CV9......2 C1
Haunchwood Park Dr
 NUNW/HART CV10......22 D3
Haunchwood Rd
 NUNW/HART CV10......24 A3
Hawk Cl NUN CV11......37 H2
Hawkesbury La COVE CV2......45 H3
Hawkins Cl HINC LE10......8 C5
Hawley Rd HINC LE10......18 B5
Hawthorn Crs HINC LE10......28 D3
Hawthorne Av
 RCOVN/BALC/EX CV7......33 F2
Hawthorne Ter
 NUNW/HART CV10......24 C2
Hawthorne Wy RLEIW/BAR LE9......9 C3
Haydock Cl COVN CV6......45 F4
Hayes Green Rd
 RCOVN/BALC/EX CV7......40 D4
Hayes La RCOVN/BALC/EX CV7......40 D5
Hayes Rd NUNW/HART CV10......13 F4
Hayle Cl NUN CV11......26 B2
Hays La HINC LE10......18 A5
Hazel Cl NUNW/HART CV10......13 F5
Hazel Gv BDWTH CV12......41 H2
Hazell Wy NUNW/HART CV10......36 A1
Hazel Rd NUNW/HART CV10......24 A2
Hazel Wy RLEIW/BAR LE9......9 F2
Heath Av BDWTH CV12......40 C4
Heath End Rd NUNW/HART CV10 ...24 B5
Heather Cl NUNW/HART CV10......24 C4
Heather Dr BDWTH CV12......40 C3
Heath La RLEIW/BAR LE9......9 H1
Heath La South RLEIW/BAR LE9 ...10 A2
Heathley La BDWTH CV12......40 D4
Hebden Wy NUN CV11......26 B5
Heckley Rd RCOVN/BALC/EX CV7 .45 E1
The Hedgerows
 NUNW/HART CV10......24 C1
Helena Cl NUNW/HART CV10......24 C4
Helston Cl NUN CV11......26 A2
Hemdale NUN CV11......26 B5
Hemsworth Dr BDWTH CV12......42 D3
Hen La COVN CV6......44 B5
Henley Cl NUN CV11......16 A4
Henry St HINC LE10......17 H2
 NUN CV11......25 E5
Henson Rd BDWTH CV12......40 C4
Henson Wy HINC LE10......31 E3
Herald Wy HINC LE10......28 C2
Herbert St NUNW/HART CV10......24 B4
Hereford Cl NUNW/HART CV10......24 B3
 RLEIW/BAR LE9......9 E2
Hereford Rd NUN CV11......38 D4
Herford Wy HINC LE10......29 E1
Herring Rd ATHST CV9......2 D4
Heyford Cl COVE CV2......45 H5
Hickman Rd NUNW/HART CV10......23 F3
Hidcote Cl NUN CV11......37 F2
Higham La HINC LE10......17 F1
 MKTBOS/BARL/STKG CV13......6 D3
 NUN CV11......25 H1
Higham Wy HINC LE10......18 D5
High Ash Cl RCOVN/BALC/EX CV7 .44 D1
Highbury Gn NUNW/HART CV10 ...13 H5
Highfield Rd NUN CV11......25 G5
Highfields Rd HINC LE10......18 D3
Highfield St RLEIW/BAR LE9......10 A3
 RLEIW/BAR LE9......21 G2
High St BDWTH CV12......41 F3
 MKTBOS/BARL/STKG CV13......7 E2
 NUN CV11......25 E3
 RLEIW/BAR LE9......9 E3
 RLEIW/BAR LE9......10 C2
High Tor East RLEIW/BAR LE9......10 B3
High Tor West RLEIW/BAR LE9......10 B3
High View Dr
 RCOVN/BALC/EX CV7......44 A1
Hilary Bevins Cl
 MKTBOS/BARL/STKG CV13......6 A3
Hilary Rd NUNW/HART CV10......24 B2
Hillcrest Rd NUNW/HART CV10......24 A2
Hill Farm Av NUN CV11......37 H1
Hilliard Cl BDWTH CV12......41 E1
Hillrise HINC LE10......19 E4
Hillside NUNW/HART CV10......13 F4
Hillside Dr NUNW/HART CV10 ...13 H5

Hillside Rd HINC LE10......28 B1
Hill St BDWTH CV12......36 B5
 HINC LE10......18 C4
 NUNW/HART CV10......24 A3
 RLEIW/BAR LE9......9 G3
Hill Top RLEIW/BAR LE9......10 C1
Hilton Av NUNW/HART CV10......23 G1
Himley Rd BDWTH CV12......40 B3
Hinckley La
 MKTBOS/BARL/STKG CV13......16 C1
Hinckley Rd HINC LE10......19 F5
 HINC LE10......20 A5
 MKTBOS/BARL/STKG CV13......7 C1
 NUN CV11......25 H2
 NUN CV11......39 E2
 RLEIW/BAR LE9......8 D3
 RLEIW/BAR LE9......10 A3
 RLEIW/BAR LE9......20 D5
Hoarestone Av NUN CV11......37 G3
Hogarth Cl BDWTH CV12......41 E1
 HINC LE10......17 H1
Hogarth Dr HINC LE10......17 H1
Holbein Cl BDWTH CV12......41 E1
Hollick Crs RCOVN/BALC/EX CV7 .33 E2
Hollier's Wk HINC LE10......18 C3
Hollinwell Cl NUN CV11......38 A2
The Hollow RLEIW/BAR LE9......10 C2
Hollybush La COVN CV6......45 E4
Holly Cl HINC LE10......28 D2
Hollycroft HINC LE10......18 A2
Hollycroft Crs HINC LE10......18 B2
Hollydene Crs RLEIW/BAR LE9......10 A3
Hollyhurst BDWTH CV12......40 D4
Holly La ATHST CV9......2 B2
 RLEIW/BAR LE9......9 G2
Holly Stitches Rd
 NUNW/HART CV10......24 B1
Holly Wk NUN CV11......26 A5
Holman Wy NUN CV11......25 G4
Holsworthy Cl NUN CV11......25 H2
Holte Rd ATHST CV9......2 C2
Holt Rd HINC LE10......18 C5
Holyoak Cl BDWTH CV12......40 B4
Holyoak Dr HINC LE10......31 E3
Home Farm Cl ATHST CV9......3 G3
Home Park Rd NUN CV11......25 F4
Homestead Houses
 RLEIW/BAR LE9 *......31 H1
Horobins Yd BDWTH CV12 *......41 F1
The Horsefair HINC LE10......18 C4
Horsepool HINC LE10......29 F2
Horse Shoe Rd COVN CV6......45 H4
Hosiery St BDWTH CV12......41 G3
Houldsworth Crs COVN CV6......44 A4
Howard Cl RLEIW/BAR LE9......9 F2
Howard Rd NUNW/HART CV10......24 D4
Howe Cl RLEIW/BAR LE9......21 F4
Howells Cl BDWTH CV12......40 B5
Hoylake Cl NUN CV11......37 H1
Humphrey-Davy Rd
 BDWTH CV12......40 B5
Huncote Rd RLEIW/BAR LE9......21 G1
Hunters La
 MKTBOS/BARL/STKG CV13......4 D3
Hunters Wk ATHST CV9......3 G4
Huntingdon Wy
 NUNW/HART CV10......24 B4
Hunt La ATHST CV9......3 G4
Hurn Wy COVN CV6......45 F4
Hurst Rd BDWTH CV12......41 F2
 COVN CV6......45 F4
 HINC LE10......18 C4
 RLEIW/BAR LE9......10 B3
Hyacinth Wy HINC LE10......28 C2
Hydes La HINC LE10......27 E3

Ibstock Rd COVN CV6......45 E3
Ilford Cl BDWTH CV12......40 D2
Ilminster Cl HINC LE10......19 G5
Inchford Cl NUN CV11......37 F1
Ingleton Cl NUN CV11......26 B5
Innage Ter ATHST CV9 *......2 C3
Iris Cl HINC LE10......28 D2
Ironbridge Wy COVN CV6......44 D3
Isambard Dr COVN CV6......44 D3
Island Cl HINC LE10......18 D2
Ivanhoe Av NUN CV11......37 F1
Ivor Rd ATHST CV9......3 G4
Ivy Cl MKTBOS/BARL/STKG CV13 ...7 C1
Ivydene Cl RLEIW/BAR LE9......10 C2
Ivy Gv NUNW/HART CV10......24 A1

Jacker's Rd COVN CV6......45 F4
Jacknell Rd HINC LE10......17 E4
James St NUN CV11......24 D2
 RCOVN/BALC/EX CV7......33 E2
 RLEIW/BAR LE9......10 B3
Jarvis Cl HINC LE10......8 C5
Jefferies Cl HINC LE10......18 C2
Jeffrey Cl BDWTH CV12......40 B5
Jellicoe Wy HINC LE10......8 C5
Jersey Wy RLEIW/BAR LE9......9 F3
Jodrell St NUN CV11......25 E2
John Bold Av RLEIW/BAR LE9......21 H2
John Knight Rd BDWTH CV12......36 B5
John Nichols St HINC LE10......18 A5
John's Cl HINC LE10......28 C2
John Shelton Dr COVN CV6......44 A4
Johnson Ri RLEIW/BAR LE9......21 H3
Johnson Rd BDWTH CV12......41 G2
John St BDWTH CV12......41 E3
 HINC LE10......18 D3
 NUN CV11......25 F5
 NUNW/HART CV10......24 B4
Jon Baker Ct HINC LE10......18 D4
Jones Rd RCOVN/BALC/EX CV7 ...41 E4
Joseph Luckman Rd
 BDWTH CV12......41 E1
Jovian Dr HINC LE10......17 H3
Jubilee Dr RLEIW/BAR LE9......21 G1
Jubilee Ter BDWTH CV12 *......41 F1
Judd Cl BDWTH CV12......40 D2
Judds La COVN CV6......44 C4
Juliet Cl NUN CV11......37 G1
Juniper Cl BDWTH CV12......40 B3

Kanzan Rd COVE CV2......45 G4
Karen Cl NUNW/HART CV10......14 B5
Kathleen Av BDWTH CV12......40 C4
Katrine Cl NUNW/HART CV10......23 H2
Keats Cl NUNW/HART CV10......23 F2
 RLEIW/BAR LE9......10 C1
Keats La RLEIW/BAR LE9......10 B1
Keenan Dr BDWTH CV12......40 B4
Keepers Wk BDWTH CV12 *......40 B4
Kegworth Cl COVN CV6......45 E4
Kelsey Cl NUN CV11......25 H4
Kem St NUN CV11......25 H5
Kendal Cl NUN CV11......26 B3
Kendrick Cl COVN CV6......45 E4
Kenilworth Dr NUN CV11......24 C4
Kenmore Dr HINC LE10......18 A2
Kennel La ATHST CV9......3 G4
Kensington Cl NUNW/HART CV10 .23 H1
Kensington Ct NUNW/HART CV10 .23 H1
Kent Dr HINC LE10......8 D5
Kerry Cl RLEIW/BAR LE9......9 F2
Kestrel Cl HINC LE10......29 E1
Keswick Cl NUN CV11......26 B1
Kielder Dr NUNW/HART CV10......24 B5
Kilby Gn HINC LE10......29 E1
Kilmarie Cl HINC LE10......17 H3
Kiln Cl NUNW/HART CV10......24 B4
Kimberley Rd BDWTH CV12......41 F1
King Edward Rd NUN CV11......25 E3
King George's Av BDWTH CV12 ...36 B5
King George's Wy HINC LE10......18 A5
King Richard Rd HINC LE10......18 C4
King Richard's Hl RLEIW/BAR LE9 .11 E1
Kings Av ATHST CV9......2 D1
Kingsbridge Rd
 NUNW/HART CV10......25 G1
Kings Ct NUN CV11 *......25 E3
 RLEIW/BAR LE9 *......9 G2
Kingsfield Rd RLEIW/BAR LE9......9 G2
Kings Gdns BDWTH CV12......41 G3
Kingsley Crs BDWTH CV12......42 D3
Kingston Dr HINC LE10......8 D5
King St BDWTH CV12......41 G3
 RLEIW/BAR LE9......9 G3
King's Wk RLEIW/BAR LE9......10 B2
Kingsway NUN CV11......25 E3
Kingswood Rd NUNW/HART CV10 .23 H3
Kinross Cl NUNW/HART CV10......24 C5
Kinross Wy HINC LE10......17 G3
Kintyre Cl HINC LE10......18 A3
Kipling Cl NUNW/HART CV10......23 F2

Kirby Cl RLEIW/BAR LE9......21
Kirfield Dr HINC LE10......19
Kirkby Rd RLEIW/BAR LE9......9
Kirkdale Av COVN CV6......44
Kirkstone Rd BDWTH CV12......41
Klevedon Cl NUN CV11......37
Knapton Dr HINC LE10......17
Knebley Crs NUNW/HART CV10......36
Knightsbridge Av BDWTH CV12......36
Knights Cl HINC LE10......28
 RLEIW/BAR LE9......21
Knights Link RLEIW/BAR LE9......11
Knowles Av NUNW/HART CV10......23
Knox Crs NUN CV11......16

Laburnum Cl BDWTH CV12......40
Laburnum Dr RLEIW/BAR LE9......10
Laburnum Gv NUNW/HART CV10 ...24
Lady La COVN CV6......44
Lady Warwick Av BDWTH CV12......41
Laggan Cl NUNW/HART CV10......23
Lakeside BDWTH CV12......41
Lamford Cl HINC LE10......17
Lamorna Cl NUN CV11......26
Lamp La RCOVN/BALC/EX CV7......32
Lancaster Cl ATHST CV9......2
Lancaster Rd HINC LE10......18
Lance Cl HINC LE10......28
Lancia Cl COVN CV6......45
Lancing Rd BDWTH CV12......43
Landseer Dr HINC LE10......17
Land Society La RLEIW/BAR LE9 ...10
Lanes Hill Gv RLEIW/BAR LE9......21
Laneside Dr HINC LE10......19
Langdale Av COVN CV6......44
Langdale Cl NUN CV11......26
Langdale Rd HINC LE10......17
Lansdowne Cl BDWTH CV12......41
The Larches RCOVN/BALC/EX CV7 .41
Larchwood Rd
 RCOVN/BALC/EX CV7......
Larkin Cl BDWTH CV12......42
Lauderdale Av COVN CV6......
Launceston Dr NUN CV11......26
Laurel Dr NUNW/HART CV10......13
The Laurels BDWTH CV12......40
Lavender Cl BDWTH CV12......40
Lavenham Cl NUN CV11......38
The Lawns BDWTH CV12......40
 HINC LE10......18
Lawnswood HINC LE10......17
Lawton Cl HINC LE10......17
Laxford Cl HINC LE10......17
Leam Cl NUN CV11......3
Leas Cl BDWTH CV12......3
Leathermill La NUNW/HART CV10 ..14
Leaward Cl NUNW/HART CV10......26
Lee Cl RLEIW/BAR LE9......2
The Leecrofts RLEIW/BAR LE9......10
Lees High HINC LE10......3
Leicester Ct BDWTH CV12......43
Leicester Crs ATHST CV9......
Leicester Rd BDWTH CV12......4
 HINC LE10......18
 HINC LE10......19
 HINC LE10......3
 NUN CV11......3
 RLEIW/BAR LE9......3
Leicester St BDWTH CV12......4
 BDWTH CV12......
Leighton Crs RLEIW/BAR LE9......1
Lenton's La COVE CV2......
Leven Cl HINC LE10......1
Lewis Ct ATHST CV9......
Leyburn Cl COVN CV6......4
 NUN CV11......
Leyland Rd BDWTH CV12......4
 NUN CV11......
Liberty Wy NUN CV11......
Library Cl HINC LE10......
Lichfield Cl NUN CV11......
 RCOVN/BALC/EX CV7......3
Lilac Cl HINC LE10......
Lilac Rd BDWTH CV12......
Lime Gv NUNW/HART CV10......
 RLEIW/BAR LE9......
Limes Coppice NUNW/HART CV10 .1
The Limes BDWTH CV12......4
Lincoln Av NUNW/HART CV10......
Lincoln Rd HINC LE10......
Linden Lea BDWTH CV12......
Linden Rd HINC LE10......

...dley Rd *BDWTH* CV12 ....40 B3
...gwood Dr *NUNW/HART* CV10 ...24 C4
...stock Wy *COVN* CV6 ....45 F4
...wood Cl *HINC* LE10 ....17 H2
...keard Cl *NUN* CV11 ....26 B2
...more Dr *HINC* LE10 ....18 A3
...ter St *ATHST* CV9 ....2 C2
...ter St *NUN* CV11 ....25 G4
...le Duke St *NUN* CV11 ....25 E3
...esey Dr *RLEIW/BAR* LE9 ....31 F1
...yd Cl *NUN* CV11 ....25 G5
...ach Dr *COVE* CV2 ....45 F4
...chmore Cl *HINC* LE10 ....17 H4
...chmore Dr *HINC* LE10 ....17 H4
...chmore La *HINC* LE10 ....17 H4
...dge Cl *ATHST* CV9 ....3 F5
...HINC LE10 ....29 F3
...e Cl *COVN* CV6 ....45 E4
...mond Cl *HINC* LE10 ....18 A4
...mond Wy *NUNW/HART* CV10 ...23 H2
...don Rd *HINC* LE10 ....18 D4
...gford Rd
  RCOVN/BALC/EX CV7 ....45 E2
...gford Sq *COVN* CV6 ....44 D4
...e Long Shoot *NUN* CV11 ....26 C1
...g St *ATHST* CV9 ....2 B2
...BDWTH CV12 ....43 F3
...RLEIW/BAR LE9 ....21 H2
...siemouth Rd *HINC* LE10 ....17 G3
...reday Cl *ATHST* CV9 ....2 C1
...elace Crs *RLEIW/BAR* LE9 ....10 C5
...re La *HINC* LE10 ....29 F1
...ell Cl *RCOVN/BALC/EX* CV7 ....41 E5
...ell Rd *BDWTH* CV12 ....41 E2
...etts Rd *HINC* LE10 ....17 C4
...wer Bond St *HINC* LE10 ....18 C3
...weswater Cl *NUN* CV11 ....26 B1
...wry Cl *BDWTH* CV12 ....41 E1
...as Rd *HINC* LE10 ....28 C1
...as Wy *RLEIW/BAR* LE9 ....10 B3
...erne Cl *COVE* CV2 ....45 G5
...ilford Rd *NUNW/HART* CV10 ....22 A3
...ilford Rd *NUNW/HART* CV10 ....23 H1
...idy Cl *HINC* LE10 ....18 A3
...in Cl *HINC* LE10 ....28 C1
...terworth Rd *HINC* LE10 ....29 C3
...NUN CV11 ....25 H5
...hgate Cl *HINC* LE10 ....29 F2
...hgate La *HINC* LE10 ....29 G2
...ington Dr *COVN* CV6 ....45 F2
...e Lynch *NUN* CV11 ....25 C5
...dene Cl *RLEIW/BAR* LE9 ....9 H1
...dhurst Cl *COVN* CV6 ....45 F3
...HINC LE10 ....29 F1
...eham Cl *HINC* LE10 ....17 H1
...mouth Cl *NUN* CV11 ....25 H2

M

...gee Cl *HINC* LE10 ....18 B2
...gyar Crs *NUN* CV11 ....37 F2
...n St *MKTBOS/BARL/STKG* CV13 ...7 F2
...MKTBOS/BARL/STKG CV13 ....16 A1
...zefield *HINC* LE10 ....18 B1
...ham Cl *NUN* CV11 ....26 B5
...lard Av *NUNW/HART* CV10 ......23 H2
...lard Dr *HINC* LE10 ....17 H5
...lerin Cft *NUNW/HART* CV10 ....23 G2
...lory St *RLEIW/BAR* LE9 ....9 H1
...lory Wy *RCOVN/BALC/EX* CV7 ..44 C3
...thouse Cl *NUNW/HART* CV10 ...22 A3
...e Maltings *NUN* CV11 * 25 H2
...vern Av *NUNW/HART* CV10 ......23 G2
...ncetter Rd *ATHST* CV9 ....3 F5
...NUNW/HART CV10 ....14 A4
...ndarin Cl *HINC* LE10 ....27 H1
...nor Cl *HINC* LE10 ....28 B2
...nor Court Av *NUN* CV11 ....25 E2
...nor Court Rd *NUN* CV11 ....24 D3
...nor House Cl *HINC* LE10 ....30 B3
...nor Park Rd *NUN* CV11 ....24 D2
...nor Pl *HINC* LE10 ....18 B3
...nor Rd *ATHST* CV9 ....2 D5
...LEIW/BAR LE9 ....21 G5
...nor St *HINC* LE10 ....18 B3
...nor Wy *HINC* LE10 ....28 C2
...nse Ct *RCOVN/BALC/EX* CV7 ....41 E4
...nsion St *HINC* LE10 ....18 B4
...ole Av *RCOVN/BALC/EX* CV7 ....41 F4
...ole Cl *HINC* LE10 ....28 C2
...ole Rd *NUNW/HART* CV10 ....24 B2
...e Maples *BDWTH* CV12 ....40 C4
...ole Wy *RLEIW/BAR* LE9 ....10 A4

Marchant Rd *HINC* LE10 ....18 B4
Marchfont Cl *NUN* CV11 ....26 A5
Margaret Av *BDWTH* CV12 ....41 E2
Margaret Rd *ATHST* CV9 ....2 C4
Marie Cl *ATHST* CV9 ....3 F4
Marigold Cl *BDWTH* CV12 ....28 D2
Market End Cl *BDWTH* CV12 ......40 A3
Market Pl *HINC* LE10 ....18 C4
Market St *ATHST* CV9 ....2 C3
Marlborough Cl *HINC* LE10 ....19 G5
Marlborough Rd *NUN* CV11 ....25 E2
Marlowe Cl *NUNW/HART* CV10 ..23 E2
Marlwood Cl *COVN* CV6 ....44 D4
Marner Rd *BDWTH* CV12 ....41 E2
  NUN/HART CV10 ....36 B1
Marriott Rd *BDWTH* CV12 ....40 B3
Marsdale Dr *NUNW/HART* CV10 ..24 B4
Marshall Rd *RCOVN/BALC/EX* CV7 ..41 F5
Marsdale La *COVN* CV6 ....44 C5
Marston La *BDWTH* CV12 ....40 B1
  NUN CV11 ....37 E2
Martin Cl *RLEIW/BAR* LE9 ....21 G4
Martindale Rd
  RCOVN/BALC/EX CV7 ....41 G5
Martins Dr *ATHST* CV9 ....3 E2
Martins Rd *BDWTH* CV12 ....40 C4
Marwood Cl *NUN* CV11 ....37 E3
Maryland Cl *RLEIW/BAR* LE9 ....9 H3
Mary St *RLEIW/BAR* LE9 ....10 C2
Marywell Cl *HINC* LE10 ....17 G3
Masefield Cl *RLEIW/BAR* LE9 ....9 G1
Mason Ct *HINC* LE10 ....18 A4
Masser Rd *COVN* CV6 ....44 A4
Maughan St *RLEIW/BAR* LE9 .....10 C1
Mavor Dr *BDWTH* CV12 ....40 B4
Mawnan Cl *RCOVN/BALC/EX* CV7 ..41 F5
Mayfair Dr *NUNW/HART* CV10 ...23 E3
Mayfield Cl *BDWTH* CV12 ....41 F2
Mayfield Rd *NUN* CV11 ....25 H5
Mayfield Wy *RLEIW/BAR* LE9 ....9 H2
Maynard Av *BDWTH* CV12 ....40 B5
Mays Farm Dr *RLEIW/BAR* LE9 ..21 G2
McDonnell Dr
  RCOVN/BALC/EX CV7 ....44 D2
McMahon Rd *BDWTH* CV12 ....40 C5
Meadow Cl *HINC* LE10 ....21 G2
Meadow Ct *NUN* CV11 ....25 E3
Meadow Court Rd
  RLEIW/BAR LE9 ....10 C3
Meadow Cft
  RCOVN/BALC/EX CV7 ....32 C1
Meadow Dr *HINC* LE10 ....19 F5
Meadow Rd *NUNW/HART* CV10 ..13 F4
  RLEIW/BAR LE9 ....9 H2
Meadowside *NUN* CV11 ....37 H2
The Meadows *HINC* LE10 ....19 F5
Meadow St *ATHST* CV9 ....2 C3
  NUN CV11 ....25 E3
The Meadway *HINC* LE10 ....19 G5
Melbourne Cl *NUN* CV11 ....37 E2
Meldrum Rd *NUNW/HART* CV10 ..24 A4
Melfort Cl *NUNW/HART* CV10 ....23 G2
Melrose Av *BDWTH* CV12 ....40 B5
Melrose Cl *HINC* LE10 ....18 A4
Melton St *RLEIW/BAR* LE9 ....10 B2
Melville Cl *RCOVN/BALC/EX* CV7 ..41 E5
Mendip Dr *NUNW/HART* CV10 ...23 G4
Merevale Av *HINC* LE10 ....18 B5
  NUN CV11 ....24 D3
Merevale Cl *HINC* LE10 ....18 B5
Merevale Rd *ATHST* CV9 ....2 B2
Merevale Vw *ATHST* CV9 ....2 B1
Merlin Av *NUNW/HART* CV10 .....23 G1
Merrifield Gdns *HINC* LE10 ....28 D2
Mersey Rd *BDWTH* CV12 ....42 C3
Metcalf Cl *RLEIW/BAR* LE9 ....21 G3
Metcalfe St *RLEIW/BAR* LE9 ......10 B3
The Mews *BDWTH* CV12 ....41 F3
Middleburg Cl *NUN* CV11 ....37 G2
Middlefield Cl *HINC* LE10 ....18 C2
Middlefield Ct *HINC* LE10 ....18 C2
Middlefield La *HINC* LE10 ....18 C1
Middlefield Pl *HINC* LE10 ....18 C1
Middlemarch Rd
  NUNW/HART CV10 ....36 B1
Middleton Cl *RLEIW/BAR* LE9 ....21 H3
Midland Rd *NUN* CV11 ....24 D3
Milby Dr *NUN* CV11 ....16 A4
Milfoil Cl *HINC* LE10 ....17 G5
Milford Rd *NUNW/HART* CV10 ...25 E5
Millais Cl *BDWTH* CV12 ....41 E1
Mill Cl *COVE* CV2 ....45 F5
  NUN CV11 ....37 F1
  RLEIW/BAR LE9 ....21 H5
Millers Gn *HINC* LE10 ....29 E1
Mill Hill Rd *HINC* LE10 ....18 B3
Milliners St *ATHST* CV9 ....2 C3
Mill La *ATHST* CV9 ....3 F3
  BDWTH CV12 ....42 C2

HINC LE10 ....31 F3
  NUN CV11 ....38 D2
  RCOVN/BALC/EX CV7 ....32 A5
  RLEIW/BAR LE9 ....10 D1
Mill Race La *COVN* CV6 ....45 E5
Mill Race Vw *ATHST* CV9 ....2 C1
Mill St *BDWTH* CV12 ....41 F2
  NUN CV11 ....25 F3
  RLEIW/BAR LE9 ....9 E4
Mill Ter *BDWTH* CV12 ....36 B5
Mill Vw *HINC* LE10 ....18 D3
Mill Wk *NUN* CV11 ....25 F3
Milner Cl *BDWTH* CV12 ....43 F3
Milton Cl *BDWTH* CV12 ....41 H4
  HINC LE10 ....18 B3
Minions Cl *ATHST* CV9 ....2 C3
Mira Dr
  MKTBOS/BARL/STKG CV13 .....15 F1
Mistral Cl *HINC* LE10 ....19 E4
Mitchell Rd *BDWTH* CV12 ....41 E1
Moat Farm Dr *BDWTH* CV12 ......40 A5
Moat Wy *RLEIW/BAR* LE9 ....9 E3
Mona St *RLEIW/BAR* LE9 ....10 B3
Monmouth Gdns
  NUNW/HART CV10 ....24 B3
Montana Wk *NUNW/HART* CV10 ..24 B4
Montgomery Rd *RLEIW/BAR* LE9 ..10 D2
Montrose Dr *NUNW/HART* CV10 ..24 C4
Moorbrooke *NUNW/HART* CV10 ..13 F5
Moorcroft Cl *NUN* CV11 ....37 H1
Moore Cl *COVN* CV6 ....45 E4
Moore Rd *RLEIW/BAR* LE9 ....9 G2
Moorpark Cl *NUN* CV11 ....38 A2
Moor Rd *NUNW/HART* CV10 ......13 F4
Moorwood Crs
  NUNW/HART CV10 ....13 F4
Moorwood La *NUNW/HART* CV10 ..13 F4
Moray Cl *HINC* LE10 ....17 H4
Morgan Cl *RCOVN/BALC/EX* CV7 ..32 D2
Morland Cl *BDWTH* CV12 ....43 F3
Morland Dr *HINC* LE10 ....18 A1
Morland Rd *COVN* CV6 ....44 A5
Morley Rd *RLEIW/BAR* LE9 ....31 H1
Morris Dr *NUN* CV11 ....36 D1
Mortiboys Wy *RLEIW/BAR* LE9 ..21 G3
Mossdale Crs *NUNW/HART* CV10 ..24 C5
Mount Av *RLEIW/BAR* LE9 ....9 H2
Mount Dr *BDWTH* CV12 ....40 B5
Mountfield Rd *RLEIW/BAR* LE9 ..10 B2
Mount Pleasant Rd *BDWTH* CV12 ..41 E2
Mount Pleasant Ter
  NUNW/HART CV10 ....24 C1
Mount Rd *HINC* LE10 ....18 C4
Mount St *NUN* CV11 ....25 E3
Muirfield Cl *NUN* CV11 ....38 A2
Mulberry Wy *NUNW/HART* CV10 ..13 E4
Munnings Dr *HINC* LE10 ....17 H1
Myrtle Cl *RLEIW/BAR* LE9 ....9 F3
Mythe La *ATHST* CV9 ....3 F3
Mythe Vw *ATHST* CV9 ....2 D2

N

Nairn Cl *NUNW/HART* CV10 ....24 D5
Neale Cl *BDWTH* CV12 ....43 E4
Nelson Dr *HINC* LE10 ....8 C5
Netherley Rd *HINC* LE10 ....18 C1
Neville Smith Cl *RLEIW/BAR* LE9 ..31 G1
Newcomen Cl *BDWTH* CV12 ......40 B5
Newcomen Rd *BDWTH* CV12 .....40 B4
New Cottages
  NUNW/HART CV10 * 24 C4
Newdegate Rd *BDWTH* CV12 .....41 E1
Newdegate St *NUN* CV11 ....25 F3
Newey Av *BDWTH* CV12 ....40 B5
Newham Gn *NUNW/HART* CV10 ..13 H5
Newlands Rd *RLEIW/BAR* LE9 ......9 G2
Newlyn Cl *NUN* CV11 ....26 A3
Newman Cl *BDWTH* CV12 ....41 F1
Newmarket Cl *COVN* CV6 ....45 F4
Newquay Cl *HINC* LE10 ....26 A2
  NUN CV11 ....26 A2
New Rd *HINC* LE10 ....29 F1
  RLEIW/BAR LE9 ....21 H3
Newstead Av *HINC* LE10 ....28 D3
Newstead Cl *NUN* CV11 ....26 A5
New St *BDWTH* CV12 ....41 G3
  BDWTH CV12 ....43 E3
  HINC LE10 ....18 C3
  RLEIW/BAR LE9 ....10 B2
Newton Cl *NUNW/HART* CV10 ...13 G2
Newton Rd *HINC* LE10 ....18 D1
Newtown Rd *BDWTH* CV12 ....40 D3
  NUN CV11 ....25 F2

New Wk *RLEIW/BAR* LE9 ....31 G1
Nightingale Cl *ATHST* CV9 ....2 D2
Niton Rd *NUNW/HART* CV10 ......25 G1
Nock Verges *RLEIW/BAR* LE9 ....10 D1
  RLEIW/BAR LE9 ....21 G3
Nolan Cl *COVN* CV6 ....44 B3
The Nook *NUN* CV11 ....25 H5
Norfolk Cl *HINC* LE10 ....28 C3
Norfolk Crs *NUNW/HART* CV10 ..24 B4
Norman Av *NUN* CV11 ....25 E3
Norman Dagley Cl
  RLEIW/BAR LE9 ....10 B3
Normandy Wy *HINC* LE10 ....17 G3
North Av *BDWTH* CV12 ....41 H3
Northbourne Dr *NUN* CV11 ....37 F3
North Cl *HINC* LE10 ....28 D1
Northcote Wk *ATHST* CV9 ....2 C1
Northfield Rd *HINC* LE10 ....18 A5
Northleigh Wy *RLEIW/BAR* LE9 ..10 C3
North St *ATHST* CV9 ....2 C3
  NUNW/HART CV10 ....24 C4
Northumberland Av
  NUNW/HART CV10 ....24 B4
Norton Rd *RLEIW/BAR* LE9 ....9 H1
Norwich Cl *NUN* CV11 ....16 B4
Nuffield Rd *HINC* LE10 ....17 F5
Nuneaton La
  MKTBOS/BARL/STKG CV13 .....16 A2
Nuneaton Rd *BDWTH* CV12 ....37 H5
  BDWTH CV12 ....41 F1
  NUNW/HART CV10 ....13 H2
Nursery Gdns *RLEIW/BAR* LE9 ..10 A3
Nursery Rd *ATHST* CV9 ....3 E4
  NUN/HART CV10 ....12 D4
Nuthurst Crs *NUNW/HART* CV10 ..22 B4
Nuthurst La *NUNW/HART* CV10 ..22 B5
Nutt's La *HINC* LE10 ....27 G1

O

Oak Cl *BDWTH* CV12 ....41 G1
  HINC LE10 ....28 D2
Oakdale Rd *RLEIW/BAR* LE9 ......10 A3
Oakdene Crs *NUNW/HART* CV10 ..15 C5
Oakey Cl *COVN* CV6 ....44 D4
Oakfield Gdns *ATHST* CV9 ....2 D4
Oakham Crs *BDWTH* CV12 ....43 F3
Oakmoor Rd *COVN* CV6 ....45 E5
Oakroyd Crs *NUNW/HART* CV10 ..14 A5
Oaks Pl *COVN* CV6 ....45 E5
The Oaks *BDWTH* CV12 ....40 D4
Oaks Wy *RLEIW/BAR* LE9 ....10 B2
Oaston Rd *NUN* CV11 ....25 G3
Oban Dr *NUNW/HART* CV10 ......24 D5
Oban Rd *COVN* CV6 ....44 D3
  HINC LE10 ....17 H5
Oberon Cl *NUN* CV11 ....37 G1
Odstone Dr *HINC* LE10 ....17 G4
Oldany Wy *NUNW/HART* CV10 ...24 C5
Oldbury Rd *NUNW/HART* CV10 ..12 B3
Oldbury Vw *NUNW/HART* CV10 ..13 G3
Old Crown Ms *COVE* CV2 ....45 H3
Old Farm Rd *ATHST* CV9 ....3 E5
Old Forge Rd
  MKTBOS/BARL/STKG CV13 ....4 D3
Old Hinckley Rd
  NUNW/HART CV10 ....25 G2
Old Holly La *ATHST* CV9 ....2 B1
Old Meeting Yd *BDWTH* CV12 * ..41 F2
Olton Cl *NUN* CV11 ....39 E2
Olton Pl *NUNW/HART* CV10 ......24 C3
Orchard Cl *ATHST* CV9 ....3 G3
  HINC LE10 ....29 F2
  NUNW/HART CV10 ....13 F5
Orchard Ct *ATHST* CV9 ....2 C4
Orchard St *BDWTH* CV12 ....36 B5
  HINC LE10 ....18 D4
  NUN CV11 ....25 G3
The Orchard *RLEIW/BAR* LE9 ....21 H3
Orchard Wy *NUNW/HART* CV10 ..23 H1
Orford Ri *NUNW/HART* CV10 .....22 D3
Orkney Cl *HINC* LE10 ....18 A3
  NUNW/HART CV10 ....24 D5
Ormond Cl *RLEIW/BAR* LE9 ....9 F2
Orpington Dr *COVN* CV6 ....44 B4
Orton Rd *COVN* CV6 ....44 A5
Orwell Cl *NUNW/HART* CV10 .....23 F2
Osbaston Cl *HINC* LE10 ....19 E1
Osprey Cl *NUN* CV11 ....37 H2
Outlands Dr *HINC* LE10 ....17 H2
Outwoods Cl *ATHST* CV9 ....2 B4
The Oval *RLEIW/BAR* LE9 ....21 H3
Owen St *ATHST* CV9 ....2 C3
Oxford Cl *NUN* CV11 ....16 A4

Oxford St *RLEIW/BAR* LE9 ....9 G2
   RLEIW/BAR LE9 ....10 C2

P

Packwood Cl *NUN* CV11 ....37 F2
Paddiford Pl *NUNW/HART* CV10 ....23 H4
The Paddocks *BDWTH* CV12 ....42 D2
Padstow Cl *NUN* CV11 ....26 A2
Paget Ct *COVE* CV2 ....45 F5
Pallett Dr *NUN* CV11 ....16 B5
Palmer Rd *HINC* LE10 ....18 A2
The Parade *NUN* CV11 ....25 F4
Paragon Wy
   RCOVN/BALC/EX CV7 ....41 F5
Park Av *COVN* CV6 ....44 A5
   NUN CV11 ....25 H4
Park Cl *RLEIW/BAR* LE9 ....10 B1
Parkinson Dr *ATHST* CV9 ....2 D1
Parkland Cl *COVN* CV6 ....44 A5
Park La *NUNW/HART* CV10 ....23 E3
   RCOVN/BALC/EX CV7 ....33 E5
Park Rd *BDWTH* CV12 ....41 H4
   HINC LE10 ....18 D4
   RLEIW/BAR LE9 ....10 C2
   RLEIW/BAR LE9 ....31 G1
Park St *NUN* CV11 ....25 G4
Park Vw *HINC* LE10 ....31 E4
Park View Cl
   RCOVN/BALC/EX CV7 ....45 E1
Parkville Cl *COVN* CV6 ....44 A5
Parrotts Gv *COVE* CV2 ....45 H3
Parson's La *HINC* LE10 ....18 D4
Peake Av *NUN* CV11 ....15 H4
Pear Tree Av *NUNW/HART* CV10 ....24 B1
Pear Tree Cl *RLEIW/BAR* LE9 ....9 G1
Pebblebrook Wy *BDWTH* CV12 ....41 G3
Peckleton Gn *RLEIW/BAR* LE9 ....9 G1
Peggs Cl *RLEIW/BAR* LE9 ....10 C2
Pembroke Cl *BDWTH* CV12 ....40 D1
Pembroke Wy *NUN* CV11 ....25 G4
Pembury Av *COVN* CV6 ....45 E5
Penfold Cl *RLEIW/BAR* LE9 ....21 G5
Pennant Rd *HINC* LE10 ....28 C2
Pennine Wy *NUNW/HART* CV10 ....23 G4
Penny La *RLEIW/BAR* LE9 ....9 F3
Penryn Cl *NUN* CV11 ....26 B2
Penshurst Wy *NUN* CV11 ....37 F2
Pentire Cl *NUN* CV11 ....25 H2
Pentland Cl *HINC* LE10 ....18 A4
Penzance Cl *HINC* LE10 ....8 D5
Penzance Wy *NUN* CV11 ....26 A2
Peter's Cl *RLEIW/BAR* LE9 ....21 F3
Peters Wk *COVN* CV6 ....45 E4
Pheasant Cl *BDWTH* CV12 ....40 B4
Pickford Cl *NUN* CV11 ....37 G1
Pike Cl *HINC* LE10 ....28 C2
Pine Cl *MKTBOS/BARL/STKG* CV13....7 F2
The Pines *BDWTH* CV12 ....40 C3
Pine Tree Rd *BDWTH* CV12 ....41 G1
Pingle Cl *NUN* CV11 ....25 G1
Pingle La *RLEIW/BAR* LE9 ....11 H3
Pipers La *NUNW/HART* CV10 ....12 B4
Plough Hill Rd *NUNW/HART* CV10..23 E1
Pool Bank St *NUN* CV11 ....25 E3
Pool Rd *NUNW/HART* CV10................24 C2
Poplar Av *BDWTH* CV12 ....41 H3
The Poplars *NUNW/HART* CV10 ....24 A4
   RLEIW/BAR LE9 ....10 D1
Portia Cl *NUN* CV11 ....37 G2
Portland Dr *HINC* LE10 ....18 D1
   NUNW/HART CV10 ....23 H3
Post Office La *ATHST* CV9 ....3 G4
Potters Rd *BDWTH* CV12 ....40 B4
Pougher Cl *RLEIW/BAR* LE9 ....31 H1
Powell Wy *NUN* CV11 ....25 E3
Powers Rd *HINC* LE10 ....9 E4
Poyser Rd *NUNW/HART* CV10 ....36 C2
Prescelly Cl *NUNW/HART* CV10 ....23 G4
Preston Rd *HINC* LE10 ....18 A2
Priesthills Rd *HINC* LE10 ....18 C4
Primrose Dr *BDWTH* CV12 ....40 C4
   HINC LE10 ....28 D2
Prince's Av *NUN* CV11 ....25 E4
Princess Rd *ATHST* CV9 ....2 D3
   HINC LE10 ....18 D4
Prince's St *NUN* CV11 ....25 E4
The Priors *BDWTH* CV12 ....41 G1
Priory St *NUNW/HART* CV10 ....23 H4
Priory Wk *ATHST* CV9 ....3 E5
   HINC LE10 ....18 D3
Prospect Wy *RLEIW/BAR* LE9 ....10 B2
Ptarmigan Pl *NUN* CV11 ....26 A4
Pughe's Cl *HINC* LE10 ....29 F1

Purcell Av *NUN* CV11 ....37 G3
Purley Chase La *ATHST* CV9 ....12 B1
Purley Vw *ATHST* CV9 ....3 E5
Pyeharps Rd *HINC* LE10 ....28 D2

Q

Quaker Cl
   MKTBOS/BARL/STKG CV13 ....4 D3
Quantock Dr *NUNW/HART* CV10 ....23 G4
Quarry La *NUN* CV11 ....37 F1
Quarry Yd *NUNW/HART* CV10 * 23 H4
Queen Elizabeth Rd
   NUNW/HART CV10 ....23 H1
Queen Mary's Rd *BDWTH* CV12 ....36 C5
Queens Ar *NUN* CV11 * 25 F3
Queens Ct *NUN* CV11 * 24 D3
Queens Rd *ATHST* CV9 ....2 D3
   HINC LE10 ....18 D4
   NUN CV11 ....24 D3
Queen St *BDWTH* CV12 ....41 G1
   RLEIW/BAR LE9 ....9 G3
Queensway *NUNW/HART* CV10 ....25 G1
   RLEIW/BAR LE9 ....9 H2

R

Racemeadow Rd *ATHST* CV9 ....3 E2
Radford Cl *ATHST* CV9 ....2 D1
Radley Dr *NUNW/HART* CV10 ....36 A1
Radmore Rd *HINC* LE10 ....18 C1
Radnor Dr *NUNW/HART* CV10 ....24 B5
Raglan Cl *NUN* CV11 ....26 A5
Ragley Wy *NUN* CV11 ....26 A5
Railway Ter *ATHST* CV9 * 2 C3
   CV12 * 41 G1
Rainsbrook Dr *NUN* CV11 ....37 G1
Raison Av *NUN* CV11 ....16 A4
Raleigh Cl *HINC* LE10 ....8 C5
Ramsden Av *NUNW/HART* CV10 ....13 H5
Ramsden Ct *NUNW/HART* CV10 * ..13 H5
Ramsden Rd *ATHST* CV9 ....3 F4
Ramsey Cl *HINC* LE10 ....18 A3
Randle Rd *NUNW/HART* CV10 ....24 A3
Rannoch Cl *HINC* LE10 ....18 A4
Rannoch Dr *NUNW/HART* CV10 ....23 H2
Ransome Rd
   RCOVN/BALC/EX CV7 ....33 E2
Ratcliffe Br *ATHST* CV9 ....3 E1
Ratcliffe Rd *ATHST* CV9 ....2 D3
   HINC LE10 ....29 E1
Ratcliffe St *ATHST* CV9 ....2 C3
Raveloe Dr *NUN* CV11 ....36 D1
Raven Wy *NUN* CV11 ....26 A5
Rawn Vw *ATHST* CV9 ....3 G1
Raymond Cl *COVN* CV6 ....44 D3
Raynor Crs *BDWTH* CV12 ....40 B4
The Raywoods
   NUNW/HART CV10 ....24 C4
Reading Av *NUN* CV11 ....16 A4
Reading Cl *COVE* CV2 ....45 F5
Recreation Rd *COVN* CV6 ....45 E5
Rectory Cl *RCOVN/BALC/EX* CV7 ..41 E4
Rectory Cottages
   RCOVN/BALC/EX CV7 * 32 C1
Rectory Dr *RCOVN/BALC/EX* CV7 ..41 E4
Rectory Rd *RCOVN/BALC/EX* CV7 ..32 C1
Redcap Cft *COVN* CV6 * 44 B4
Red Deeps *NUN* CV11 ....36 D1
Red Hall Dr *RLEIW/BAR* LE9 ....9 G2
Red Hall Rd *RLEIW/BAR* LE9 ....9 H2
Red La *NUNW/HART* CV10 ....34 A3
Redruth Cl *NUN* CV11 ....26 A3
Redwood Cft *NUNW/HART* CV10...24 D5
Reeves Rd *HINC* LE10 ....29 E1
Regency Cl *NUNW/HART* CV10 ....25 G1
Regent St *BDWTH* CV12 ....41 G1
   HINC LE10 ....18 C4
   NUN CV11 ....25 G3
   RLEIW/BAR LE9 ....9 G2
Renison Rd *BDWTH* CV12 ....40 C4
Repington Av *ATHST* CV9 ....3 F3
Reynolds Cl *HINC* LE10 ....17 H1
Reynolds Rd *BDWTH* CV12 ....41 H1
Rhyl Rd *NUN* CV11 ....38 D4
Ribble Cl *BDWTH* CV12 ....42 D3
Ribblesdale Av *HINC* LE10 ....18 A1
Ribbonfields *NUN* CV11 ....25 G4
Richardson Cl *RLEIW/BAR* LE9 ....21 G4

Richmond Rd *ATHST* CV9 ....2 C4
   HINC LE10 ....18 B1
   NUN CV11 ....24 D4
Riddon Dr *HINC* LE10 ....18 A4
The Ridgeway *HINC* LE10 ....28 C1
Riley Cl *RLEIW/BAR* LE9 ....21 G4
The Rills *HINC* LE10 ....18 D2
River Cl *RCOVN/BALC/EX* CV7....40 D4
River Dr *ATHST* CV9 ....2 C1
Rivermead *NUN* CV11 ....24 D3
Riversdale Rd *ATHST* CV9 ....3 E3
Riverside *ATHST* CV9 ....3 F4
Riversley Rd *NUN* CV11 ....25 F4
Roanne Ringway *NUN* CV11 ....25 F3
Robert Rd *RCOVN/BALC/EX* CV7 ..40 D5
Robertson Cl *RLEIW/BAR* LE9....21 G3
Robinson Rd *BDWTH* CV12 ....40 B5
Robinson Wy *HINC* LE10 ....29 E3
Robins Wy *NUNW/HART* CV10 ....23 F4
Rochester Cl *NUNW/HART* CV10 ..25 E4
Rock Cl *NUNW/HART* CV10 ....23 E5
Rockingham Dr *NUN* CV11................37 F3
Rodney Cl *HINC* LE10 ....8 C5
Rogue's La *HINC* LE10 ....7 H4
Roland Mt *COVN* CV6 ....44 A5
Rollasons Yd *COVN* CV6 * 45 E5
Roman Cl *RLEIW/BAR* LE9 * 10 D1
Romney Cl *HINC* LE10 ....17 H1
Romsey Av *NUNW/HART* CV10...15 G4
Ronald Toon Rd *RLEIW/BAR* LE9 ...10 D2
Rookery Cl
   MKTBOS/BARL/STKG CV13 ....4 D2
The Rookery *NUNW/HART* CV10 ...22 D2
Rose Hl *ATHST* CV9 ....2 A4
Rose La *NUN* CV11 ....25 F4
Rosemary Wy *HINC* LE10 ....18 A5
Rosemullion Cl
   RCOVN/BALC/EX CV7 ....41 F5
Roseway
   MKTBOS/BARL/STKG CV13 ....7 E3
Rosewood *NUN* CV11 ....37 F1
Rosewood Cl *HINC* LE10 ....28 C5
Rossendale Rd *RLEIW/BAR* LE9 ....10 A2
Rossendale Wy
   NUNW/HART CV10 ....24 A5
Ross Wy *NUN* CV11 ....37 H3
Roston Dr *HINC* LE10 ....17 G4
Rothesay Cl *NUNW/HART* CV10...24 D5
The Roundhills *RLEIW/BAR* LE9 ....10 C5
Rowan Rd *NUNW/HART* CV10 ....23 H1
The Rowans *BDWTH* CV12 ....40 C3
Rowland Ct *RCOVN/BALC/EX* CV7..32 C1
Rowley's Green La *COVN* CV6 ....44 C4
Roxburgh Rd *NUN* CV11 ....37 E1
Royal Cl *HINC* LE10 ....18 B5
Royal Meadow Dr *ATHST* CV9 ....2 D1
Royal Oak La
   RCOVN/BALC/EX CV7 ....44 A1
Royal Oak Yd *BDWTH* CV12 * 45 E4
Rudgard Rd *COVN* CV6 ....45 E4
Rufford Cl *HINC* LE10 ....28 C4
Rugby Rd *BDWTH* CV12 ....43 E3
   HINC LE10 ....18 B5
Runneymede Gdns
   NUNW/HART CV10 ....24 C4
Ruskin Cl *NUNW/HART* CV10 ....23 F2
Rutherford Gln *NUN* CV11 ....37 F1
Rutland Cl *HINC* LE10 ....18 B5
   NUNW/HART CV10 ....24 C3
Rydal Av *NUN* CV11 ....26 B1
Rydal Cl *HINC* LE10 ....17 G5
Ryde Av *NUNW/HART* CV10 ....25 G1
Ryder Rw *RCOVN/BALC/EX* CV7...33 E2
Ryders Hill Crs *NUNW/HART* CV10..13 H5
Rye Piece Ringway *BDWTH* CV12...41 G1
Ryhope Cl *BDWTH* CV12 ....40 A4

S

Saddlers Cl *HINC* LE10 ....29 E1
Sadler Gdns *BDWTH* CV12 ....41 G3
Saffron Cl *RLEIW/BAR* LE9 ....9 H1
St Agnes Wy *NUN* CV11 ....26 A3
St Andrews Dr *NUN* CV11 ....37 G1
St Austell Cl *NUN* CV11 ....26 B2
St Benedicts Cl *ATHST* CV9 ....2 C3
St Catherine's *HINC* LE10 ....19 E5
St Davids Wy *NUNW/HART* CV10..36 A4
St Francis Cl *HINC* LE10 ....18 B1
St George's Av *HINC* LE10 ....18 B5
St George's Rd *ATHST* CV9 ....2 C1
St Georges Wy
   NUNW/HART CV10 ....36 B2
St Giles Rd *RCOVN/BALC/EX* CV7..44 B2

St Helen's Cl *HINC* LE10 31
St Ives Wy *NUN* CV11 26
St James's Cl *HINC* LE10 28
St Johns Cl *NUNW/HART* CV10 12
St Lawrence Rd
   NUNW/HART CV10 22
St Lukes Wy *NUNW/HART* CV10 23
St Margaret Rd
   MKTBOS/BARL/STKG CV13 7
St Marks Cl *NUNW/HART* CV10 23
St Martin's *HINC* LE10 28
St Mary's Av *RLEIW/BAR* LE9 9
St Mary's Ct *RLEIW/BAR* LE9 9
St Mary's Rd *ATHST* CV9 2
   HINC LE10 18
   NUN CV11 25
St Michaels Cl *ATHST* CV9 3
   RCOVN/BALC/EX CV7 32
St Michael's Wy
   NUNW/HART CV10 23
St Nicolas Park Dr *NUN* CV11....15
St Nicolas Rd *NUN* CV11 25
St Paul's Rd *NUNW/HART* CV10 ...23
St Peter's Av *ATHST* CV9 3
St Peter's Cl *ATHST* CV9 3
St Peter's Dr *NUNW/HART* CV10 ...3
St Peters Rd *ATHST* CV9 3
Saints Wy *NUNW/HART* CV10 25
St Thomas' Rd *COVN* CV6 44
St Thomass Cl
   NUNW/HART CV10 23
Salcombe Cl *NUN* CV11 26
Salem Rd *HINC* LE10 29
Salisbury Dr *NUNW/HART* CV10...13
Salisbury Rd *HINC* LE10 19
Sanby Cl *BDWTH* CV12 41
Sanders Cl *ATHST* CV9 2
Sanders Rd *COVN* CV6 45
Sandford Cl *COVE* CV2 45
   HINC LE10 19
Sandon Rd *NUN* CV11 25
Sandpiper Rd *COVE* CV2 45
Sandringham Av *RLEIW/BAR* LE9 ..10
Sandy Crs *HINC* LE10 18
Sapcote Gv *COVN* CV6 45
Sapcote Rd *HINC* LE10 19
   RLEIW/BAR LE9 9
Saunders Av *BDWTH* CV12 41
Saville Cl *HINC* LE10 18
School Cl *HINC* LE10 28
School Hl *NUNW/HART* CV10 13
School La *HINC* LE10 31
   NUNW/HART CV10 22
   RCOVN/BALC/EX CV7 44
School Rd *BDWTH* CV12 43
School Wk *NUN* CV11 25
Scott Av *NUNW/HART* CV10 15
Seaford Cl *COVN* CV6 45
Seaforth Dr *HINC* LE10 17
Sealand Dr *BDWTH* CV12 40
Seaton Cl *HINC* LE10 19
   NUN CV11 26
Seeswood Cl *NUNW/HART* CV10 ...23
Selby Wy *NUNW/HART* CV10 24
Selworthy Rd *COVN* CV6 44
Sennen Cl *NUN* CV11 26
Sephton Dr *COVN* CV6 45
Severn Av *HINC* LE10 19
Severn Rd *BDWTH* CV12 42
Sewage Cottages
   NUNW/HART CV10 * 13
Seymour Rd *NUN* CV11 25
Shackleton Dr *HINC* LE10 28
Shadrack Cl *RLEIW/BAR* LE9 21
Shakespeare Av *BDWTH* CV12 41
Shakespeare Dr *HINC* LE10 18
   NUN CV11 37
Shanklin Dr *NUNW/HART* CV10 ...25
Sharnbrook Gdns *HINC* LE10 31
Sharnford Rd *HINC* LE10 30
   RLEIW/BAR LE9 30
Sharpless Rd *HINC* LE10 18
Sharratt Rd *BDWTH* CV12 41
Shawe Av *NUNW/HART* CV10 15
Sheepy Cl *HINC* LE10 19
Shelley Cl *BDWTH* CV12 41
Shelley Gdns *HINC* LE10 18
Shenton Cl
   MKTBOS/BARL/STKG CV13 9
Shenton Rd *RLEIW/BAR* LE9 9
Shepperton St *NUN* CV11................25
Sherborne Rd *HINC* LE10 19
Sherbourne Av
   NUNW/HART CV10 23
Sheridan Dr *NUNW/HART* CV10 ...23
Sheringham Cl *NUN* CV11 26
Sherwood Rd
   MKTBOS/BARL/STKG CV13 9
Shetland Dr *NUNW/HART* CV10 ...24

illingstone Dr
NUNW/HART CV10 ....24 C5
ilton La *BDWTH* CV12 ....43 F4
ilton Rd *RLEIW/BAR* LE9 ....9 C3
irlett Cl *COVN* CV6 ....45 F4
pesmith Cl *RLEIW/BAR* LE9 ......9 F3
ortlands *RCOVN/BALC/EX* CV7 ..44 B2
ort St *NUNW/HART* CV10 ....23 H3
rewsbury Cl *RLEIW/BAR* LE9 ......9 F2
mouth Cl *NUN* CV11 ....26 A2
ver Birch Av *BDWTH* CV12 ......40 C3
verbirch Cl *NUNW/HART* CV10 ...13 H5
verdale Cl *COVE* CV2 ....45 F4
verstone Dr
RCOVN/BALC/EX CV7 ....44 C3
ver Wk *NUNW/HART* CV10 ....24 C4
mmonds Wy *ATHST* CV9 ....2 C1
ley Wy *HINC* LE10 ....17 H1
elwith Ri *NUN* CV11 ....26 B1
etchley Hall Gdns *HINC* LE10 ...28 C4
etchley La *HINC* LE10 ....28 B2
etchley Manor La *HINC* LE10 ....28 C2
etchley Mdw *HINC* LE10 ....28 B2
etchley Old Village *HINC* LE10 ..28 B2
ve Cl *NUNW/HART* CV10 ....24 C3
de Cl *NUN* CV11 ....38 A2
ath's Yd *BDWTH* CV12 ....41 F2
dmere Cl *COVE* CV2 ....45 F5
ets Yd *BDWTH* CV12 ....41 E3
gsby Cl *NUN* CV11 ....25 H5
arts Rd *BDWTH* CV12 ....40 D4
ercote Cl *BDWTH* CV12 ....40 B4
ith St *BDWTH* CV12 ....40 C4
ths Yd *BDWTH* CV12 * 41 F1
ithy Farm Dr *RLEIW/BAR* LE9 ...21 F3
ithy La *HINC* LE10 ....19 H4
orrall La *BDWTH* CV12 ....40 B4
owdon Cl *NUNW/HART* CV10 ......23 G4
owshill Cl *NUN* CV11 ....37 F2
ar Wy *HINC* LE10 ....17 H4
merset Dr *NUNW/HART* CV10 .....24 D3
rell Pl *NUNW/HART* CV10 ....36 D2
rell Rd *NUNW/HART* CV10 ....36 C2
th Dr *RLEIW/BAR* LE9 ....21 H4
thfield Cl *NUNW/HART* CV10 .....25 G1
thfield Rd *HINC* LE10 ....18 C5
thlands *ATHST* CV9 ....2 D4
th St *ATHST* CV9 2
Cl *HINC* LE10 ....18 D3
Dr *RLEIW/BAR* LE9 ....21 G5
La *HINC* LE10 ....18 D3
ncer St *HINC* LE10 ....18 C3
Spindles *HINC* LE10 ....29 E2
nney Cl *RCOVN/BALC/EX* CV7 ...32 C2
nney La *NUNW/HART* CV10 ....23 H3
nney Rd *HINC* LE10 ....28 B1
Spinney *ATHST* CV9 ....3 F4
Spires *NUNW/HART* CV10 ....23 H3
ngdale Ct *NUN* CV11 * 25 G4
ngfield Crs *BDWTH* CV12 ....41 F2
ngfield Rd *HINC* LE10 ....18 C5
UN CV11 ....25 H5
nghill *NUNW/HART* CV10 ....13 F4
ng Hl *RCOVN/BALC/EX* CV7 ......32 D3
ng Hill Rd *NUNW/HART* CV10 ....23 H1
Square *NUN* CV11 ....25 H5
ires Gn *HINC* LE10 ....29 E1
Stables *HINC* LE10 ....28 C2
ole Wk *NUN* CV11 ....26 A5
ford Cl *BDWTH* CV12 ....43 E3
ford St *ATHST* CV9 ....2 C4
LEIW/BAR LE9 ....9 F3
nes Cl *NUN* CV11 ....16 A5
nforth Cl *NUN* CV11 ....26 A1
nford Cl *NUN* CV11 * 25 E2
nford Ct *NUN* CV11 * 25 E2
nley Rd *ATHST* CV9 ....2 C4
HINC LE10 ....18 B2
UN CV11 ....24 D2
nley St *RLEIW/BAR* LE9 ....9 F3
nton La *RLEIW/BAR* LE9 ....21 E5
nton Rd *RLEIW/BAR* LE9 ....21 E2
LEIW/BAR LE9 ....21 G5
les Cl *BDWTH* CV12 ....43 E3
leton La
KTBOS/BARL/STKG CV13 ....7 G1
LEIW/BAR LE9 ....9 E1
Cottages *RLEIW/BAR* LE9 * 21 E2
tin Rd *RCOVN/BALC/EX* CV7 .....44 D1
ion Rd *HINC* LE10 ....18 C4
KTBOS/BARL/STKG CV13 ....6 A5
KTBOS/BARL/STKG CV13 ....6 D2
COVN/BALC/EX CV7 ....32 B2
LEIW/BAR LE9 ....10 B4
LEIW/BAR LE9 ....20 D1
LEIW/BAR LE9 ....21 F2
ion St *ATHST* CV9 ....2 C3

Stephenson Rd *HINC* LE10 ....17 F5
Sterling Wy *NUN* CV11 ....37 F1
Sterling Wy *NUN* CV11 ....37 F1
Stevens Cl *RLEIW/BAR* LE9 ......21 H3
Stewart Ct
RCOVN/BALC/EX CV7 * 33 E2
Stewart St *NUN* CV11 ....25 E4
Stirling Av *HINC* LE10 ....17 H3
Stockwell Head *HINC* LE10 ....18 C3
Stoke La *HINC* LE10 ....7 G5
MKTBOS/BARL/STKG CV13 ....6 C5
MKTBOS/BARL/STKG CV13 ....7 F1
Stoke Rd *HINC* LE10 ....8 A5
MKTBOS/BARL/STKG CV13 ....7 G2
Stokesay Cl *NUNW/HART* CV10 ...24 D4
Stonebrook Wy *COVN* CV6 ....44 D5
Stonehouse La
RCOVN/BALC/EX CV7 ....32 B3
Stoneleigh Cl *NUNW/HART* CV10 ..13 G2
Stoneley Rd
MKTBOS/BARL/STKG CV13 ....7 G5
Stonewell Crs *NUN* CV11 ....37 H2
Stoneycroft Rd *RLEIW/BAR* LE9 ..10 A3
Stoneygate Dr *HINC* LE10 ....18 D1
Stoney Rd *NUNW/HART* CV10 .....25 E1
Stratford Av *ATHST* CV9 ....2 B4
Strathmore Rd *HINC* LE10 ....17 H5
Stretton Cl *HINC* LE10 ....28 C1
Stretton Rd *NUNW/HART* CV10 ...24 D4
Stroma Wy *NUNW/HART* CV10 ....24 C5
Strutt Rd *HINC* LE10 ....29 F2
Stubbs Cl *BDWTH* CV12 ....41 E1
Sudeley Rd *NUNW/HART* CV10 ....36 C2
Suffolk Cl *BDWTH* CV12 ....40 D2
NUNW/HART CV10 ....24 B4
Sunart Wy *NUNW/HART* CV10 .....23 H2
Sunningdale Cl *NUN* CV11 ....37 G1
Sunnydale Crs *HINC* LE10 ....17 H5
Sunnydale Rd *HINC* LE10 ....17 G5
Sunnyhill *HINC* LE10 ....19 E5
Sunnyhill South *HINC* LE10 ......19 E5
Sunnyside *HINC* LE10 ....18 C1
Sunnyside Ct
NUNW/HART CV10 * 24 C4
Surrey Cl *HINC* LE10 ....28 C2
Sussex Cl *NUNW/HART* CV10 .....24 B4
Sutherland Dr *BDWTH* CV12 ......41 E1
Sutton Cl *HINC* LE10 ....19 E1
Sutton Stop *COVN* CV6 ....45 F3
Swains Gn *HINC* LE10 ....29 E1
Swinburne Cl *NUNW/HART* CV10 ..23 F2
Swinburne Rd *HINC* LE10 ....18 A3
Sword Dr *HINC* LE10 ....18 A1
Sycamore Cl *HINC* LE10 ....28 D2
Sycamore Crs
RCOVN/BALC/EX CV7 ....33 F2
Sycamore Rd *NUNW/HART* CV10 ..24 A1
The Sycamores *BDWTH* CV12 .....40 C3
Sydnall Flds *COVN* CV6 ....44 D4
Sydnall Rd *COVN* CV6 ....44 D3

T

Tabeners La *ATHST* CV9 ....2 C4
Tamar Rd *BDWTH* CV12 ....42 C3
Tame Wy *HINC* LE10 ....17 H4
Tamworth Rd
RCOVN/BALC/EX CV7 ....32 B4
Tannery Cl *ATHST* CV9 ....2 D3
Tansey Crs *RLEIW/BAR* LE9 ......21 F3
Tarn Cl *BDWTH* CV12 ....41 E3
Tavistock Wy *NUN* CV11 ....25 H2
Taylors Cl *RLEIW/BAR* LE9 ....21 G3
The Tea Gdn
RCOVN/BALC/EX CV7 ....40 C5
Teal Dr *HINC* LE10 ....27 H1
Teign Bank Cl *HINC* LE10 ....18 B2
Teign Bank Rd *HINC* LE10 ....18 B1
Telford Rd *RCOVN/BALC/EX* CV7 ..41 D5
Tenby Cl *BDWTH* CV12 ....40 A4
Tenlons Rd *NUNW/HART* CV10 ....24 C5
Tennant St *NUN* CV11 ....25 H4
Tennyson Rd *HINC* LE10 ....18 A3
Tenter St *ATHST* CV9 ....2 C3
Terrace Rd *ATHST* CV9 ....2 C3
Tewkesbury Dr *BDWTH* CV12 .....41 G2
Thackeray Cl
NUNW/HART CV10 ....23 F3
Thames Rd *BDWTH* CV12 ....42 C2
Thirlmere Av *NUN* CV11 ....26 A1
Thirlmere Rd *BDWTH* CV12 ....41 E3
HINC LE10 ....17 H4
Thomas St *BDWTH* CV12 ....41 E3

Thorncliffe Wy
NUNW/HART CV10 ....12 D4
Thornfield Av
MKTBOS/BARL/STKG CV13 ....7 F2
Thornfield Wy *HINC* LE10 ....18 D4
Thornhill Dr *NUN* CV11 ....37 H2
Thorntons Wy *NUNW/HART* CV10..23 F3
Thornycroft Rd *HINC* LE10 ....18 D4
Three Pots Rd *HINC* LE10 ....28 D3
Thurlaston La *RLEIW/BAR* LE9 ...11 E1
Thurlow Cl *ATHST* CV9 ....2 C1
Tilton Rd *HINC* LE10 ....28 B2
Tintagel Wy *NUN* CV11 ....26 B2
Tintern Wy *BDWTH* CV12 ....41 G3
Tipper's Hill La
RCOVN/BALC/EX CV7 ....32 B4
Tippett Cl *NUN* CV11 ....37 G3
Tithe Cl *MKTBOS/BARL/STKG* CV13 ..7 E3
Tiverton Dr *NUN* CV11 ....25 H2
Tiveycourt Rd *COVN* CV6 ....45 E5
Toler Rd *NUN* CV11 ....25 E3
Tomkinson Rd *NUNW/HART* CV10..24 B3
Topp's Dr *BDWTH* CV12 ....40 C4
Topp's Heath *BDWTH* CV12 ....40 C4
Tower Rd *BDWTH* CV12 ....41 E3
RLEIW/BAR LE9 ....10 C1
Tower View Crs
NUNW/HART CV10 ....23 G4
Townend Rd *RLEIW/BAR* LE9 ......9 F2
Townsend Dr *NUN* CV11 ....26 A4
Townsend Rd *RLEIW/BAR* LE9 ....21 G4
Townsends Cl *NUN* CV11 ....39 E1
Trafford Cl *ATHST* CV9 ....2 C1
Trafford Dr *NUNW/HART* CV10 ...23 H1
Trafford Rd *HINC* LE10 ....18 D2
Tregorrick Rd
RCOVN/BALC/EX CV7 ....45 E1
Tregullan Rd
RCOVN/BALC/EX CV7 ....41 F5
Trelawney Rd
RCOVN/BALC/EX CV7 ....45 E1
Tremelling Wy
RCOVN/BALC/EX CV7 ....32 D2
Trenance Rd
RCOVN/BALC/EX CV7 ....45 E1
Treneere Rd
RCOVN/BALC/EX CV7 ....41 E5
Trentham Cl *NUN* CV11 ....37 F2
Trentham Rd *NUNW/HART* CV10 ..13 F2
Trent Rd *BDWTH* CV12 ....42 C3
HINC LE10 ....17 H4
NUN CV11 ....25 G2
Tresillian Rd
RCOVN/BALC/EX CV7 ....41 E5
Treviscoe Cl *RCOVN/BALC/EX* CV7..45 E1
Trevor Rd *HINC* LE10 ....18 D1
Trevose Av *RCOVN/BALC/EX* CV7 ..45 F1
Trinity Ct *HINC* LE10 ....18 B4
Trinity La *HINC* LE10 ....18 B4
Trinity Vicarage Rd *HINC* LE10 ..18 B4
Trinity Wk *NUN* CV11 ....25 G5
Troon Wy *NUN* CV11 ....28 C5
Truro Cl *NUN* CV11 ....26 A2
Tryan Rd *NUNW/HART* CV10 ......24 B3
Tuckey Cl *RLEIW/BAR* LE9 ....21 G5
Tudor Crs *ATHST* CV9 ....2 C2
Tudor Rd *HINC* LE10 ....18 B2
NUNW/HART CV10 ....23 H1
Tulliver Cl *BDWTH* CV12 ....41 F1
Tulliver Rd *NUNW/HART* CV10 ....36 C2
Tunnel Rd *NUNW/HART* CV10 .....22 B4
Turnberry Dr *NUN* CV11 ....38 C2
Turner Cl *BDWTH* CV12 ....41 E1
Turner Dr *HINC* LE10 ....17 H1
Tuttle Hl *NUNW/HART* CV10 ....24 B1
Tweedside Cl *HINC* LE10 ....19 E1
Twycross Rd *HINC* LE10 ....29 E1
Tynemouth Cl *COVE* CV2 ....45 H3

U

Ullswater Av *NUN* CV11 ....26 A1
Ullswater Cl *RLEIW/BAR* LE9 .....10 C3
Ullswater Rd *BDWTH* CV12 ....41 E3
Underwood Crs *RLEIW/BAR* LE9 ..21 H5
Underwood Dr *RLEIW/BAR* LE9 ...21 H4
Union Pl *COVN* CV6 ....44 D4
Upper Abbey St *NUN* CV11 ....25 E2
Upper Bond St *HINC* LE10 ....18 C3
Upton Dr *NUN* CV11 ....37 F3
Upton La
MKTBOS/BARL/STKG CV13 ....6 C2

V

Vale Vw *NUNW/HART* CV10 ....24 B3
Valiant Cl *HINC* LE10 ....28 D3
Valley Rd *NUNW/HART* CV10 ......23 E3
Veasey Cl *NUN* CV11 ....25 H4
Ventnor St *NUNW/HART* CV10 ....25 F1
Venture Ct *HINC* LE10 ....17 F4
Vernons La *NUNW/HART* CV10 ....24 C3
Verona Cl *NUN* CV11 ....37 G1
Vicarage Cl *ATHST* CV9 ....2 D4
Vicarage La *RCOVN/BALC/EX* CV7..44 B3
Vicarage St *NUN* CV11 ....25 F3
RLEIW/BAR LE9 ....10 C2
Victoria Rd *ATHST* CV9 ....3 E5
HINC LE10 ....29 E2
NUNW/HART CV10 ....13 G4
Victoria St *HINC* LE10 ....18 D3
NUN CV11 ....25 E3
Vilia Cl *HINC* LE10 ....29 E3
Villa Cl *BDWTH* CV12 ....42 D4
Villa Crs *BDWTH* CV12 ....42 D4
Villiers St *NUN* CV11 ....25 E4
Vinecote Rd *COVN* CV6 ....44 D4
Virginia Pl *NUNW/HART* CV10 ....24 B4

W

Wadebridge Dr *NUN* CV11 ....26 A3
Wakehurst Cl *NUN* CV11 ....37 F2
Walcote Cl *HINC* LE10 ....17 G4
Walkers Wy *RCOVN/BALC/EX* CV7..40 D4
Wallingford Av *NUN* CV11 ....16 A5
Walney Cl *HINC* LE10 ....18 A3
Walnut Cl *NUNW/HART* CV10 .....13 F4
NUNW/HART CV10 ....24 B1
Walsingham Dr
NUNW/HART CV10 ....36 A4
Walter Scott Rd *BDWTH* CV12 ....41 G4
Waltham Crs *NUNW/HART* CV10 ..23 G2
Walton Cl *NUN* CV11 ....37 G3
Warwick Dr *ATHST* CV9 ....2 C1
Warwick Gdns *HINC* LE10 ....18 D1
NUNW/HART CV10 ....24 B3
Washington Cl *RLEIW/BAR* LE9 ....9 F3
Waterfall Wy *RLEIW/BAR* LE9 .....9 E4
Waterfield Wy *HINC* LE10 ....28 A2
Waterloo Rd *HINC* LE10 ....18 B4
Watersbridge Gdns
NUNW/HART CV10 ....36 C1
Waters End *RLEIW/BAR* LE9 ....9 F4
Waterside *COVN* CV6 ....45 G2
Watery Gate La *RLEIW/BAR* LE9 ..11 H2
Watling Cl *HINC* LE10 ....28 B3
Watling Dr *HINC* LE10 ....28 A3
Watling St *HINC* LE10 ....17 E5
NUN CV11 ....16 C4
NUNW/HART CV10 ....15 H2
Waveney Cl *HINC* LE10 ....17 H4
Waverley Av *NUN* CV11 ....37 F2
Waverley Sq *NUN* CV11 ....37 F2
Weaver Rd *RLEIW/BAR* LE9 ....10 C2
Webb St *NUNW/HART* CV10 ....23 H4
Webbs Wy *RLEIW/BAR* LE9 ....21 G3
Weddington La
NUNW/HART CV10 ....14 D1
Weddington Rd
NUNW/HART CV10 ....25 G2
Weddington Ter
NUNW/HART CV10 ....25 F2
Welbeck Av *HINC* LE10 ....28 C3
Welcome St *ATHST* CV9 ....2 C3
Well La *HINC* LE10 ....18 C3
Wells Cl *NUNW/HART* CV10 ....23 E3
Well Spring Cl *ATHST* CV9 ....3 E3
Welwyn Rd *HINC* LE10 ....19 E3
Wembrook Cl *NUN* CV11 ....25 G5
Wendover Dr *HINC* LE10 ....8 D5
Wenlock Wy *NUNW/HART* CV10 ..23 G3
Wensleydale Av *RLEIW/BAR* LE9 ...9 F4
Wensleydale Cl *RLEIW/BAR* LE9 ...9 F4
Wensum Cl *HINC* LE10 ....17 H4
Wentworth Cl *HINC* LE10 ....18 D1
Wentworth Dr *NUN* CV11 ....37 G1
Wesley Cl *RLEIW/BAR* LE9 ....31 H1
Wessex Cl *BDWTH* CV12 ....41 E1
West Av *BDWTH* CV12 ....41 H3
Westbury Rd *NUNW/HART* CV10 ..24 A3
West Cl *HINC* LE10 ....18 C5
Westfield Cl *NUNW/HART* CV10 ...25 G1
Westfield Rd *HINC* LE10 ....18 A5
Westminster Dr *HINC* LE10 ....29 E3

NUNW/HART CV10 ....**23** G1
Westmorland Av
  NUNW/HART CV10 ....**24** B3
Weston Cl *HINC* LE10.................**17** H3
Weston La *BDWTH* CV12.............**42** D2
Westray Dr *HINC* LE10................**18** A3
West St *RLEIW/BAR* LE9 ....**10** C1
West Vw *NUNW/HART* CV10........**12** D4
Westwood Crs *ATHST* CV9 ....**2** C4
Westwood Rd *ATHST* CV9 ....**2** C4
Wharf Cottages *ATHST* CV9 * **2** A2
Wheatfield Wy *HINC* LE10 ....**18** B1
Wheat St *NUN* CV11 ....**25** F3
Wheelwright La *COVN* CV6.........**44** A4
Whitacre Rd *NUN* CV11................**25** H2
Whitburn Rd *BDWTH* CV12...........**40** A4
Whitehall Cl *NUNW/HART* CV10....**13** F2
Whitehorse Cl *COVN* CV6............**45** F2
Whitehouse Crs
  NUNW/HART CV10 ....**24** A4
Whitemoors Cl
  MKTBOS/BARL/STKG CV13 ......**7** F2
Whitemoors Rd
  MKTBOS/BARL/STKG CV13 ......**7** F2
Whitestone Rd *NUN* CV11............**37** G3
Whitmore Park Rd *COVN* CV6......**44** A5
Whittleford Rd
  NUNW/HART CV10 ....**23** H3
Whittle Rd *HINC* LE10 ....**17** F5
Whitworth Av *HINC* LE10.............**17** G1
Wiclif Wy *NUNW/HART* CV10 ....**23** G4
Wightman Cl *RLEIW/BAR* LE9......**21** G1
Wightman Rd *RLEIW/BAR* LE9......**9** H2
Wildey Rd *BDWTH* CV12..............**40** B3
Wildmoor Cl *COVE* CV2 ....**45** F4
Wileman's Cl *RLEIW/BAR* LE9 ......**10** B4
Wilf Brown Cl *RLEIW/BAR* LE9 ......**10** D2

Willday Dr *ATHST* CV9 ....**2** C1
William Beesley Crs *NUN* CV11 ....**38** C4
William Iliffe St *HINC* LE10...........**18** A5
William St *BDWTH* CV12..............**41** H5
  NUN CV11 ....**25** H4
Willington St *NUN* CV11 * **24** D2
Willis Gv *BDWTH* CV12................**41** G2
Willowbank Rd *HINC* LE10 ....**18** B5
Willow Cl *BDWTH* CV12...............**36** A5
  HINC LE10 ....**28** D2
  NUNW/HART CV10 ....**13** F5
Willowdale *HINC* LE10.................**17** H5
Willowdene Wy *RLEIW/BAR* LE9 .....**9** G3
Willowfields Rd *NUN* CV11 ....**37** G1
Willow Rd *NUNW/HART* CV10 ......**24** B2
The Willows *ATHST* CV9 ....**2** D1
  BDWTH CV12............................**40** C3
Willow Tree Cl *RLEIW/BAR* LE9 .....**9** G1
Wilson's La *COVN* CV6.................**44** D3
  RCOVN/BALC/EX CV7 ....**45** E2
Wiltshire Cl *BDWTH* CV12............**41** E2
Wimbourne Cl *NUNW/HART* CV10...**23** F2
Winchester Av
  NUNW/HART CV10 ....**15** F4
Winchester Dr *HINC* LE10.............**19** G5
Windermere Av *NUN* CV11............**16** A5
Windermere Cl *RLEIW/BAR* LE9.....**10** C2
Winding House La *COVN* CV6........**44** B4
Windmill La *NUNW/HART* CV10 ....**34** A4
Windmill Rd *ATHST* CV9 ....**2** C2
  COVN CV6 ....**45** E5
  NUNW/HART CV10 ....**14** A5
  RCOVN/BALC/EX CV7 ....**45** E1
Windrush Dr *HINC* LE10................**17** H5
Windsor St *HINC* LE10.................**29** F2
  NUN CV11 ....**25** E3
Winfield Rd *NUN* CV11.................**25** E2

Winterborne Gdns
  NUNW/HART CV10 ....**35** H1
Winterton Rd *BDWTH* CV12..........**43** E4
Witherley Rd *ATHST* CV9 ....**3** F4
Withybrook Rd *BDWTH* CV12.........**43** G3
Woburn Cl *HINC* LE10 ....**18** D1
Woburn Dr *NUNW/HART* CV10.......**24** D5
Wolvey Rd *BDWTH* CV12..............**43** H2
  HINC LE10 ....**28** D4
Woodbank *HINC* LE10 ....**19** F5
Woodcote Av *NUN* CV11..............**16** A4
Woodfield Rd *HINC* LE10 ....**28** B1
Woodford Cl *NUNW/HART* CV10 ....**23** H3
  RCOVN/BALC/EX CV7 ....**44** B3
Woodford La *NUNW/HART* CV10....**13** G1
Woodgate Rd *HINC* LE10 ....**19** E4
Woodhall Cl *NUN* CV11................**26** A5
Woodland Av *HINC* LE10..............**29** F1
Woodland Rd *HINC* LE10...............**19** E3
Woodlands La *BDWTH* CV12.........**40** C1
Woodlands Rd *BDWTH* CV12.........**40** C2
The Woodlands
  NUNW/HART CV10 ....**13** F3
Wood La
  MKTBOS/BARL/STKG CV13 ......**15** G1
  NUNW/HART CV10 * **13** F4
Woodroffe Wk *COVN* CV6.............**45** E4
Woodshires Rd *COVN* CV6............**44** D3
Woodside *RCOVN/BALC/EX* CV7 ...**32** B1
Woodstock Cl *HINC* LE10 ....**29** F1
Woodstock Rd *NUN* CV11.............**37** E1
Wood St *BDWTH* CV12.................**41** E1
  HINC LE10 ....**18** C3
  NUNW/HART CV10 ....**24** C3
  RLEIW/BAR LE9.......................**10** B2
Wood Street Cl *HINC* LE10 ....**18** D3
Woodview Rd *ATHST* CV9...............**2** D4

Woolgrove St *COVN* CV6..............**45** ...
Woolpack Wy *ATHST* CV9 ....**2** ...
Woolwich Rd *NUN* CV11...............**38** ...
Wootton St *BDWTH* CV12.............**41** ...
Worcester Cl *RLEIW/BAR* LE9 ....**9** ...
Wordsworth Rd *BDWTH* CV12.......**41** ...
Workhouse La *HINC* LE10.............**29** ...
Wrenbury Dr *COVN* CV6................**45** ...
Wyatt Ct *BDWTH* CV12 * ....**41** ...
Wye Cl *BDWTH* CV12...................**42** ...
  HINC LE10 ....**17** ...
Wykin La
  MKTBOS/BARL/STKG CV13 ....**7** ...
Wykin Rd *HINC* LE10....................**17** ...

The Yews *BDWTH* CV12................**40** ...
Yew Tree Cl *RLEIW/BAR* LE9 ....**9** ...
York Av *ATHST* CV9 ....**2** ...
  BDWTH CV12............................**41** ...
York Rd *HINC* LE10.......................**18** ...
York St *NUN* CV11........................**24** ...

Zealand Cl *HINC* LE10..................**19** ...
Zorrina Cl *NUNW/HART* CV10 ....**23** ...

Index - featured places

Abbey CE Infant School
  NUN CV11 ....**25** E2
Abbeygate Shopping Centre
  NUN CV11 ....**25** F3
Acton Business Park
  NUNW/HART CV10 ....**24** C2
Alderman Green
  Primary School
  COVE CV2 ....**45** G5
Alderman Smith School
  NUNW/HART CV10 ....**24** A5
Alliance Business Park
  NUN CV11 ....**26** A4
All Saints CE Infant School
  BDWTH CV12............................**41** G3
All Saints CE Primary School
  NUNW/HART CV10 ....**36** C1
  RLEIW/BAR LE9.......................**31** G1
Ammond Business Centre
  NUN CV11 ....**25** H4
Arbury Hall
  NUNW/HART CV10 ....**35** E3
Arbury Medical Centre
  NUNW/HART CV10 ....**24** B4
Arden Forest Infant School
  BDWTH CV12............................**42** C2
Arden Hill Infant School
  ATHST CV9................................**2** D4
Arley Industrial Estate
  RCOVN/BALC/EX CV7 ....**32** D2
Arts Centre
  NUN CV11 ....**25** E3
Ash Green School
  RCOVN/BALC/EX CV7 ....**44** B2
Astley Castle
  NUNW/HART CV10 ....**34** A2
Astley CE School
  NUNW/HART CV10 ....**34** A3
Aston Industrial Estate
  BDWTH CV12............................**41** H3
Aston Park Industrial Estate
  NUN CV11 ....**25** E1
Atherstone College
  ATHST CV9................................**2** C3
Atherstone Golf Club
  ATHST CV9................................**2** C5
Atherstone Town Cricket Club
  ATHST CV9................................**3** E2
Atherstone United FC
  ATHST CV9................................**2** C1
Attleborough Fields
  Industrial Estate
  NUN CV11 ....**26** A4

Attleborough Sports Club
  NUN CV11 ....**25** H5
Avenue Clinic
  NUN CV11 ....**24** D2
Barwell CE Junior School
  RLEIW/BAR LE9.........................**9** F3
Barwell Infant School
  RLEIW/BAR LE9.........................**9** F3
Barwell Medical Centre
  RLEIW/BAR LE9.........................**9** F3
Battling Brook Primary School
  HINC LE10 ....**17** H2
Battling Brook Shopping Centre
  HINC LE10 ....**18** A3
Bayton Road Industrial Estate
  RCOVN/BALC/EX CV7 ....**45** F1
Bede Shopping Arcade
  BDWTH CV12............................**41** F2
Bedworth Health Centre
  BDWTH CV12............................**41** F3
Bedworth Leisure Centre
  BDWTH CV12............................**41** G3
Bedworth RFC
  BDWTH CV12............................**40** D4
Bermuda Business Park
  NUNW/HART CV10 ....**36** A3
Bermuda Park
  Industrial Estate
  NUNW/HART CV10 ....**35** H1
Bramcote Hospital
  NUN CV11 ....**38** C3
Britannia Shopping Centre
  HINC LE10 ....**18** C4
Bulkington CE Junior School
  BDWTH CV12............................**43** E3
Burbage Junior School
  HINC LE10 ....**29** F2
Camp Hill Clinic
  NUNW/HART CV10 ....**24** A1
Camp Hill Primary School
  NUNW/HART CV10 ....**24** B1
Canon Evans CE Infant School
  BDWTH CV12............................**41** E3
Canon Maggs CE Junior School
  BDWTH CV12............................**41** F3
Carlyon Road Industrial Estate
  ATHST CV9................................**3** E2
Castlemead Medical Centre
  HINC LE10 ....**18** C4
Centenary Business Centre
  NUN CV11 ....**25** H4
Centrovell Industrial Estate
  NUN CV11 ....**25** F5

Chetwynd Junior School
  NUN CV11 ....**37** F3
Chilvers Coton Community
  Infant School
  NUNW/HART CV10 ....**25** E4
Closers Business Centre
  NUN CV11 ....**25** G5
Concordia Theatre
  HINC LE10 ....**18** C3
Coventry Welsh RFC
  COVN CV6................................**44** B4
Croft Junior School
  NUNW/HART CV10 ....**24** B4
Dodwells Bridge
  Industrial Estate
  HINC LE10 ....**17** E4
Dorothy Goodman School
  HINC LE10 ....**18** C2
Etone Community School
  NUN CV11 ....**25** G2
Etone Sports Centre
  NUN CV11 ....**25** G2
Exhall Business Park
  RCOVN/BALC/EX CV7 ....**41** F5
Exhall Cedars Infant School
  RCOVN/BALC/EX CV7 ....**41** F5
Exhall Grange Special School
  RCOVN/BALC/EX CV7 ....**44** B3
Foxbank Industrial Estate
  RLEIW/BAR LE9.......................**21** G2
Foxford School
  & Community Arts College
  COVN CV6................................**45** E3
Gallagher Business Park
  RCOVN/BALC/EX CV7 ....**44** C4
Galley Common Infant School
  NUNW/HART CV10 ....**23** E2
Galley Common
  Medical Centre
  NUNW/HART CV10 ....**23** E3
The George Eliot Hospital
  NHS Trust
  NUNW/HART CV10 ....**25** E5
George Eliot School
  NUN CV11 ....**36** D1
Glendale Infant School
  NUNW/HART CV10 ....**24** C5
Goodyers End Primary School
  RCOVN/BALC/EX CV7 ....**40** C5
Grangehurst Primary School
  COVN CV6................................**45** F4
Griff Clara Industrial Estate
  NUNW/HART CV10 ....**35** H3

The Griff School
  BDWTH CV12............................**37** ...
Grovelands Industrial Estate
  RCOVN/BALC/EX CV7 ....**45** ...
Gun Hill Infant School
  RCOVN/BALC/EX CV7 ....**33** ...
Hales Industrial Park
  COVN CV6................................**44** ...
Hammond Business Centre
  NUN CV11 ....**25** ...
Hanover International
  Hotel & Club
  HINC LE10 ....**29** ...
Harrowbrook Industrial Estate
  HINC LE10 ....**17** ...
Hartshill Hayes Country Park
  NUNW/HART CV10 ....**13** ...
Hartshill School
  NUNW/HART CV10 ....**13** ...
Hastings High School
  HINC LE10 ....**19** ...
Haunchwood Park
  Industrial Estate
  NUNW/HART CV10 ....**23** ...
Hawkesbury Field School
  COVE CV2 ....**45** ...
Hawkesbury Lock
  Industrial Centre
  RCOVN/BALC/EX CV7 ....**45** ...
Hazell Way Industrial Estate
  NUNW/HART CV10 ....**35** ...
Heart of England Crematorium
  NUN CV11 ....**38** ...
Heathfield High School
  RLEIW/BAR LE9.......................**21** ...
Hemdale Business Park
  NUN CV11 ....**26** ...
Henry Bellairs CE Junior School
  BDWTH CV12............................**41** ...
Higham Lane School
  NUNW/HART CV10 ....**25** ...
Higham on the Hill CE Primary School
  MKTBOS/BARL/STKG CV13 ....**5** ...
Hijaz College
  MKTBOS/BARL/STKG CV13 .....**15** ...
Hinckley Athletic FC
  HINC LE10 ....**18** ...
Hinckley Business Centre
  HINC LE10 ....**18** ...
Hinckley Business Park
  HINC LE10 ....**29** ...
Hinckley Clinic
  HINC LE10 ....**18** ...

ckley & District Hospital
HINC LE10 ....**18** C4
ckley Golf Club
HINC LE10 ....**19** F1
ckley Health Centre
HINC LE10 ....**18** C4
ckley Sunnyside Hospital
HINC LE10 ....**8** C4
ckley Town Cricket Club
LEIW/BAR LE9 ....**9** G5
ckley Town Sports Club
LEIW/BAR LE9 ....**9** G5
iers Walk County
rimary School
HINC LE10 ....**18** C3
e Aldridge Business Centre
UNW/HART CV10 ....**25** F1
eston Grange
hopping Centre
UN CV11 ....**26** B2
n Cleveland College
HINC LE10 ....**19** F2
n Shelton Primary School
OVN CV6 ....**44** B4
lee Sports Centre
UNW/HART CV10 ....**24** D4
g Edward Business Park
UN CV11 ....**25** G3
g Edward VI College
UN CV11 ....**25** G3
s Business Centre
UN CV11 ....**25** G3
s Hotel & Restaurant
HINC LE10 ....**18** C4
Lawns Business Centre
HINC LE10 ....**18** D4
and School
DWTH CV12 ....**41** F2
gford Medical Centre
OVN CV6 ....**45** E3
gford Park Primary School
OVN CV6 ....**45** E5
orfield CE Primary School
LEIW/BAR LE9 ....**21** G3
or Park Community School
UN CV11 ....**24** D4
or Road Industrial Estate
THST CV9 ....**2** D4
se Business Centre
UN CV11 ....**25** H5
y Ann Evans Hospice
UNW/HART CV10 ....**24** D5
aael Drayton Junior School
UNW/HART CV10 ....**13** F4
dlemarch Middle School
UNW/HART CV10 ....**36** B1
y F & M Schools
UN CV11 ....**16** A4
Hill Business Centre
HINC LE10 ....**18** B4

Milverton House
Preparatory School
NUN CV11 ....**25** G4
Mirah Day Hospital
NUN CV11 ....**24** D2
Mount Grace High School
HINC LE10 ....**18** D3
Nathaniel Newton Infant School
UNW/HART CV10 ....**13** G4
Newdigate Primary School
BDWTH CV12 ....**40** A4
Newlands Primary School
RLEIW/BAR LE9 ....**9** H1
Nicholas Chamberlaine School
BDWTH CV12 ....**41** H2
North Warwickshire
& Hinckley College
ATHST CV9 ....**2** C3
HINC LE10 ....**19** E3
NUN CV11 ....**25** H1
Novotel
COVN CV6 ....**44** D2
Nuneaton Borough AFC
UNW/HART CV10 ....**24** C3
Nuneaton Co-operative
Sports Club
NUN CV11 ....**25** E3
Nuneaton Golf Club
NUN CV11 ....**38** A2
Nuneaton Indoor Market
NUN CV11 ....**25** F3
Nuneaton Museum
& Art Gallery
NUN CV11 ....**25** F4
Nuneaton Old Edwardians RFC
UNW/HART CV10 ....**25** F1
Nuneaton Private Hospital
UNW/HART CV10 ....**36** C1
Nuneaton RFC
NUN CV11 ....**26** A3
Oakfield Junior School
ATHST CV9 ....**2** D4
Oakridge Golf Club
UNW/HART CV10 ....**22** A5
Oaks Industrial Estate
RLEIW/BAR LE9 ....**10** B2
Odeon Cinema
UNW/HART CV10 ....**36** A4
Park Lane Primary School
UNW/HART CV10 ....**23** E4
Phoenix Business Park
HINC LE10 ....**17** F4
Pingles Leisure Centre
NUN CV11 ....**25** G5
Pingles Stadium
NUN CV11 ....**25** G4
Pool Road Business Centre
UNW/HART CV10 ....**24** C2
Pool Road Industrial Estate
UNW/HART CV10 ....**24** C2
Proving Ground
MKTBOS/BARL/STKG CV13 ....**6** A4

Queen Elizabeth Lower School
ATHST CV9 ....**3** E4
Queen Elizabeth Upper School
ATHST CV9 ....**2** D3
Queens CE Junior School
NUN CV11 ....**24** D3
Race Leys Primary School
BDWTH CV12 ....**41** F1
Racemeadow Primary School
ATHST CV9 ....**2** D2
Red Deeps Special School
NUNW/HART CV10 ....**36** B2
Redmoor High School
HINC LE10 ....**18** A1
The Richmond Primary School
HINC LE10 ....**18** B1
Riversley Park Clinic
NUN CV11 ....**25** F4
Rowleys Green Industrial Estate
COVN CV6 ....**44** C4
St Annes RC Primary School
NUNW/HART CV10 ....**14** A5
St Benedicts RC Primary School
ATHST CV9 ....**3** E4
St Francis RC Combined School
BDWTH CV12 ....**41** F2
St Giles Junior School
RCOVN/BALC/EX CV7 ....**40** D5
St Josephs RC First School
NUN CV11 ....**25** F4
St Margarets CE Primary School
MKTBOS/BARL/STKG CV13 ....**7** E2
St Martins RC High School
MKTBOS/BARL/STKG CV13 ....**7** G2
St Nicolas CE Primary School
NUN CV11 ....**26** A1
St Pauls CE Primary School
NUNW/HART CV10 ....**23** H4
St Peters RC Primary School
HINC LE10 ....**18** D3
RLEIW/BAR LE9 ....**10** D1
St Thomas More RC School
NUNW/HART CV10 ....**24** D4
Sharnford CE Primary School
HINC LE10 ....**31** F3
Shepperton Business Park
NUN CV11 ....**36** C1
Shilton Lane Industrial Estate
BDWTH CV12 ....**43** F5
Sketchley Grange Hotel
HINC LE10 ....**28** B3
Sketchley Hill Primary School
HINC LE10 ....**28** D2
Sketchley Lane
Industrial Estate
HINC LE10 ....**28** B2
Sketchley Meadows
Business Park
HINC LE10 ....**28** B2
Sketchley Meadows
Industrial Estate
HINC LE10 ....**28** B3

Southways Industrial Estate
HINC LE10 ....**17** F5
Spring Hill Industrial Estate
RCOVN/BALC/EX CV7 ....**32** D2
Spring Hill Medical Centre
RCOVN/BALC/EX CV7 ....**32** D3
Stockingford Clinic
NUNW/HART CV10 ....**24** A4
Stockingford Primary
& Middle School
NUNW/HART CV10 ....**24** A4
Sunnyside Industrial Estate
HINC LE10 ....**18** C1
Teal Business Park
HINC LE10 ....**17** E5
Tenlons Road Industrial Estate
NUNW/HART CV10 ....**24** C5
Three Spires Industrial Estate
....**45** E2
Townlands CE Primary School
RLEIW/BAR LE9 ....**10** C3
Travel Inn
NUNW/HART CV10 ....**36** B4
Travelodge
NUN CV11 ....**26** B1
Trident Business Park
NUN CV11 ....**25** G4
Tuttle Hill Industrial Estate
NUNW/HART CV10 ....**24** B1
Weavers Close
CE Primary School
RLEIW/BAR LE9 ....**10** C2
Weddington Industrial Estate
NUNW/HART CV10 ....**25** F2
Weddington Primary School
NUNW/HART CV10 ....**15** G5
Wembrook Primary School
NUN CV11 ....**25** F5
Westfield Infant School
HINC LE10 ....**18** A5
Westfield Junior School
HINC LE10 ....**18** A5
Weston Hall Hotel
BDWTH CV12 ....**42** D2
Whitacre Road Industrial Estate
NUN CV11 ....**25** H3
Whitestone Clinic
NUN CV11 ....**37** G2
Whitestone County
Infant School
NUN CV11 ....**37** G2
William Bradford
Community College
RLEIW/BAR LE9 ....**9** H1
Willow Park Industrial Estate
MKTBOS/BARL/STKG CV13 ....**6** C2
Witherley CE Primary School
ATHST CV9 ....**3** G4
Witherley United FC
ATHST CV9 ....**3** F3

Acknowledgements

Post Office is a registered trademark of Post Office Ltd. in the UK and other countries.

ols address data provided by Education Direct.

l station information supplied by Johnsons

way street data provided by © Tele Atlas N.V.   Tele Atlas

en centre information provided by:

en Centre Association    Britains best garden centres

vale Garden Centres

Notes

 **Street by Street** QUESTIONNAIRE

Dear Atlas User
Your comments, opinions and recommendations are very important to us.
So please help us to improve our street atlases by taking a few minutes
to complete this simple questionnaire.

You do NOT need a stamp (unless posted outside the UK). If you do not want to remove this page from your street atlas, then photocopy it or write your answers on a plain sheet of paper.

Send to: The Editor, AA Street by Street, FREEPOST SCE 4598,
Basingstoke RG21 4GY

ABOUT THE ATLAS...

Which city/town/county did you buy?

Are there any features of the atlas or mapping that you find particularly useful?

Is there anything we could have done better?

Why did you choose an AA Street by Street atlas?

Did it meet your expectations?

Exceeded ☐   **Met all** ☐   **Met most** ☐   **Fell below** ☐

Please give your reasons

continued overleaf

Where did you buy it?

For what purpose? (please tick all applicable)

To use in your own local area ☐   To use on business or at work ☐

Visiting a strange place ☐   In the car ☐   On foot ☐

Other (please state)

LOCAL KNOWLEDGE...

Local knowledge is invaluable. Whilst every attempt has been made to make the information contained in this atlas as accurate as possible, should you notice any inaccuracies, please detail them below (if necessary, use a blank piece of paper) or e-mail us at *streetbystreet@theAA.com*

ABOUT YOU...

Name (Mr/Mrs/Ms)

Address

Postcode

Daytime tel no

E-mail address

Which age group are you in?

Under 25 ☐   25-34 ☐   35-44 ☐   45-54 ☐   55-64 ☐   65+ ☐

Are you an AA member?   YES ☐   NO ☐

Do you have Internet access?   YES ☐   NO ☐

Thank you for taking the time to complete this questionnaire. Please send it to us as soon as possible, and remember, you do not need a stamp (unless posted outside the UK).

ML192